THE HIGH-IMPACT PROFESSIONAL'S PLAYBOOK

THE HIGH-IMPACT PROFESSIONAL'S PLAYBOOK

HOW TO TURN YOUR CAREER, INCOME, AND INFLUENCE INTO DOING GOOD

DEVON FRITZ

The High-Impact Professional's Playbook
How To Turn Your Career, Income, and Influence Into Doing Good

Copyright © 2025 by Devon Fritz

All rights reserved. This book or parts thereof may not be reproduced in any form without permission.

Published by Books Of Change, San Francisco

ISBN 978-1-968679-02-6

LCSH: Career development. Vocational guidance. Altruism. Charities—Decision making. Social responsibility of business.

LCC HN49.P6 2025

Book layout by Katherine Getta

Author photo by Sven Hagolani

Cover design by Trevor Messersmith

Dedication

To everyone, big or small, trying to make the world a better place.

Table Of Contents

Introduction 1
    A Life Continued 1

Chapter 1. Why Should You Want To Have an Impact? 3
    What Is Impact? 5
    Doing as Much Good as You Can 7
    The Benefactor Is Not the Recipient, or the Principal-Agent Problem 8
    ITN Framework 9
    Counterfactuality 12
    Marginal Utility 13
    A Little Bit About Values 15

Chapter 2. Causes Worth Fighting For 17
    Cause Neutrality 17
    Top Down 17
    Which Cause to Pick? An Approach 18
    Top Causes 19
    Global Health 19
    Global Development 20
    Animal Welfare 21
    Mental Health 22
    Biological Risk Mitigation 22
    Risks From Artificial Intelligence 23
    Others 24

Paths to Impact 25

Chapter 3. Your Career 27
Impact Journey Spotlight: The Counterfactual Question 28
Making an Impact Plan 29
1. Identify Your Goals 30
2. Make Options 32
3. Prioritize Your Options 33
4. Adjust Your Options 36
5. Create Your Impact Plan 37
6. Tackle Your Impact Plan 39
Start Something New 40
Volunteering 40
Personal Fit 40
Impact Journey Spotlight: The Full Circle 42
Donations vs Direct Work 43
A Quick Note About For-Profits 44
Getting Started With Career Impact 45

Chapter 4. Your Donations 47
Impact Journey Spotlight: The Intentional Earner 47
An Amazing Opportunity 48
You Are Probably Much Richer Than You Think 50
Decreasing Marginal Utility of Money 51
Giving Makes You Happier 51
Earning to Give 52
Tax Deductibility 52
Trying the Portfolio Approach 53
"Funging" and Additionality 57
Forget Overhead 58
Other Giving Mechanisms 58
Getting Started With Donations 60

Chapter 5. Workplace Initiatives 61
Impact Journey Spotlight: The Workplace Catalyst 61
Fundraising Campaigns 63
Take Advantage of Donation Matching 63
Pre-Tax Deductions of Donations Through Payroll 64
Volunteer Time Off 64
Plant-Based Lunches 64
Do Your Core Business in a More Socially Impactful Way 64
CSR Departments 64
Workplace Group 65
Summary 65
Getting Started With Workplace Initiatives 67

Chapter 6. Trusteeship 69
Impact Journey Spotlight: The Unexpected Expert 69
Getting Started as a Trustee 71

Chapter 7. Mentoring And Advisory 73
Impact Journey Spotlight: The Talent Multiplier 73
Advising a Charity 75
Mentoring an Individual 75
Getting Started With Mentoring and Advisory 77

Chapter 8. Leveraging Your Network & Influence 79
Impact Journey Spotlight: Building What's Missing 79
The Three Levels of Network Leverage 81
Fundraisers for Special Events 83
Getting Started With Influence 84

Chapter 9. Take The Next Step 85
Combine, Combine 85

Decide Which Paths to Take	85
Stay On Track With Different Accountability Mechanisms	85
Take a Mini-Pledge Right Now	86
Quick-Shot Advice For Different Barriers	86

Chapter 10. Final Thoughts 91

Appendix 93

Paths to Impact	93
Donations	94
Workplace Initiatives	94
Trustee	95
Mentoring and Advisory	95
Leveraging Your Network & Influence	95

Endnotes 97

Acknowledgements

Thank you to Nina Friedrich and Clark Wisenbaker for their contributions to this book. All mistakes are my own.

Introduction

A Life Continued

Imagine you're walking along a beach when you notice someone far from shore, arm raised weakly, clearly struggling to stay afloat. There is no lifeguard on duty.

You rush into the water.

You're a strong swimmer, and you reach them just as their strength fails. Supporting them carefully, you bring them back to shore, where they collapse in exhaustion, coughing up water but alive.

In the aftermath, you learn they were caught in a rip current that they couldn't escape. The person you saved tells you they truly thought those were their final moments—then you showed up.

If this had happened to you, it would stay with you for the rest of your life. A clear, defining moment when your direct action meant the difference between someone's life continuing or ending. It'd be something you'd likely reflect upon on your deathbed, something for which to be extremely proud.

Now consider this remarkable fact: according to a 2024 analysis by charity evaluator GiveWell[1], you can create this same outcome for a person by donating $3,000 to a highly effective charity. You can ensure a life that would have otherwise ended continues. Not metaphorically. But *actually save someone's life.*

There are other ways to do that, too. Did you know, for example, that changing your career could create a 100-fold more positive impact on the world than what you're doing now? Or that switching just 10% of your charitable giving to more effective organizations could help 100 times more lives—people or animals—with the same donation size?

These are some of the realities and opportunities of high-impact decision-making.

After a decade of helping professionals dramatically increase their positive impact on the world, I've observed a pattern emerge: many talented and successful people genuinely want to make a difference, but don't know how to go about it. So, they stay in careers that underutilize their talents for creating change. They donate ineffectively or not at all. They have large networks of highly-resourced people, but they don't—or don't know how to—leverage them.

The gap between intention and impact is costing lives. It's leaving solvable problems unsolved. And it's robbing caring professionals of the profound satisfaction that comes from knowing their work truly matters.

This book is your practical guide to closing that gap.

I've written it for busy professionals who want concrete, evidence-based strategies to maximize their impact, whether through their career, donations, side projects, or influence. I've distilled everything I've learned from my work with my organization, High Impact Professionals, focusing on actionable insights. It's the guide I wish I'd had when I first tried to align my professional life with meaningful impact.

By the time you finish reading, you'll know:

- What impact is, and how you can think about maximizing it
- About many global problems that are pressing, tractable, and neglected
- The paths to impact and what they mean for you
- Practical next steps you can take immediately, no matter your current situation

But I'll be blunt: reading this book, saying "that's interesting," and moving on without taking action is not the point. My goal isn't to inform you—it's to help you create measurable, significant, positive change in the world. It's why every section ends with specific actions you can take right away, and I genuinely hope you'll email me at hipbook@highimpactprofessionals.org to tell me which steps you've taken.

The world doesn't need more people who care. It needs people who care enough to do something about it.

Chapter 1. Why Should You Want to Have an Impact?

Countless horrific facts in this world need to be changed. More than 600,000 children die from malaria each year[2], despite those deaths being preventable for the cost of about $3,000 per person.

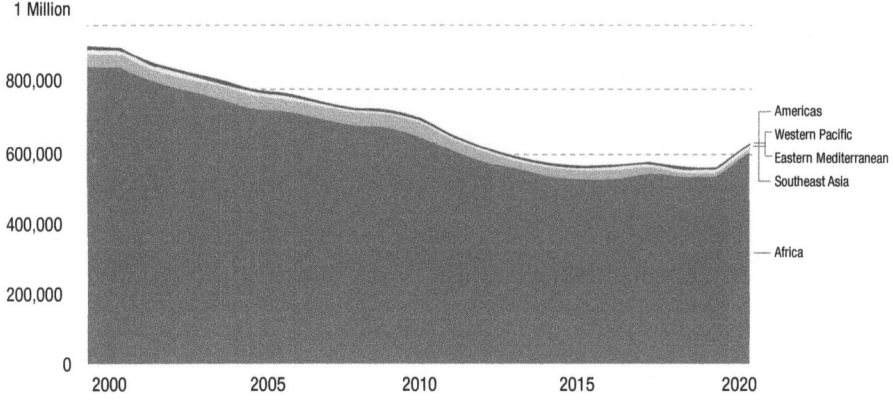

Malaria Deaths by World Region
Estimated annual number of deaths from malaria

Then there's world poverty. Over 700 million people live on less than $2.15 per day[3], with just under half the world's population living on only $6.85 per day. Or consider the fact that billions of animals suffer in factory farms under conditions we wouldn't wish on our worst enemies, and it's clear (if it wasn't already) that we live in a time of overwhelming pain and distress.

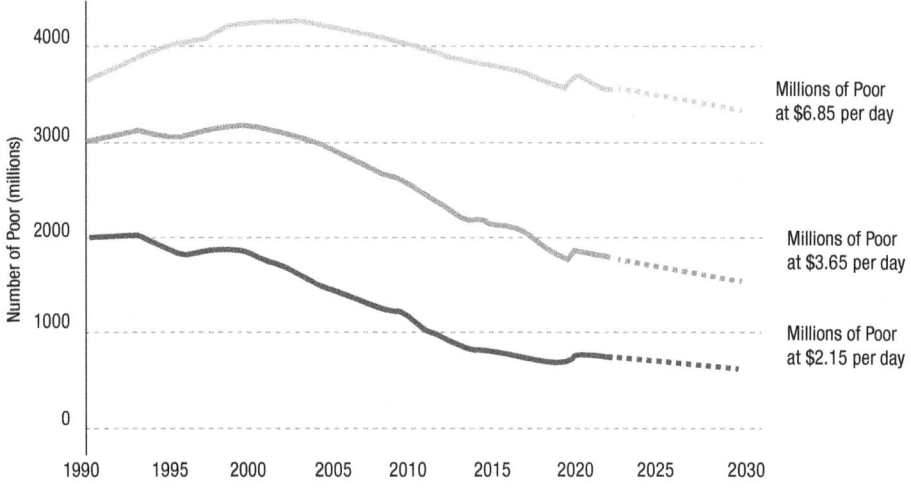

But these problems aren't unsolvable. They persist because resources and attention flow disproportionately to less effective solutions.

You have far more power to address these issues than you might realize.

And making impact a priority makes sense through multiple lenses:

It aligns with your existing values. Whether you're progressive, conservative, religious, or secular, a core part of your worldview likely includes a desire to help others lead better lives. You already care about reducing suffering and increasing flourishing. Impact-focused approaches just help you do this more effectively.

It's genuinely fulfilling. Research consistently shows that spending money and time helping others brings more lasting happiness than focusing these resources on yourself. The satisfaction from knowing your work directly saved lives or prevented suffering is profound. I've personally experienced this transformation after switching to impact-focused work (I used to build tax software!), and I'm more motivated each morning knowing my efforts matter in a measurable way.

The opportunity is unprecedented. Never before have we had such powerful tools to identify where resources can do the most good. New research, evaluation methods, and communication technologies have created a revolution in effective giving and impactful careers. Again, the difference between good and outstanding impact opportunities can be 100-fold[4], meaning your specific choices matter enormously. But choose incorrectly, and you'll leave 99 cents of every dollar on the table.

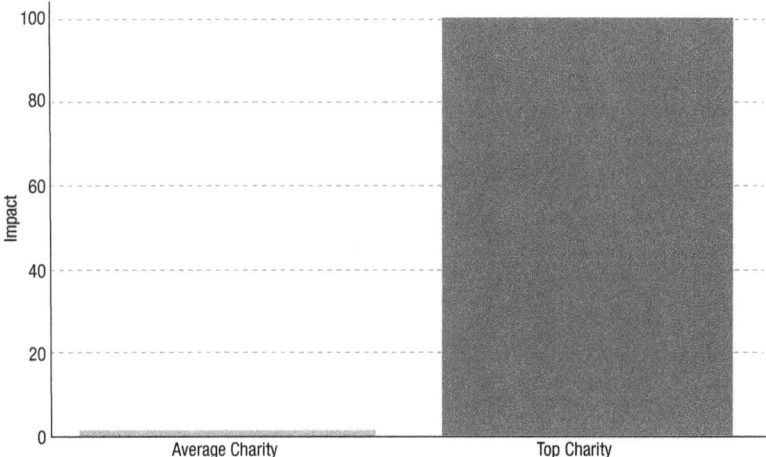

Your position is unique. If you're reading this book, you likely have education, skills, network connections, and financial resources that put you in an extremely privileged position globally. This is a grand opportunity: you have leverage that most people throughout history could only dream of. Use it!

What is Impact?

A Definition

Before exploring paths to impact, it is worthwhile to take a step back and define what we mean by **impact**. It is a word that's often overused, and it can be pretty vague if you don't nail it down. After all, a car crashing into a wall could be said to have a "big impact." That's clearly not what we mean.

While we could spend many pages on definitions and ethical frameworks, it is worth noting that I aim for this to be a practical resource; therefore, I won't delve deeply into the underlying philosophy that supports many of the thoughts presented here. If you are interested in doing that, I suggest taking the Effective Altruism Intro Program[5], an 8-week course offered by the Center for Effective Altruism.

So, what do I mean by impact? I mean **saving or improving human and animal lives.** If you reflect on the many ways you might want to make the world a better place, from averting climate change to adopting a dog from the shelter, in my experience, they will all ultimately have their true value in the above: saving or improving the lives of conscious beings. Why do we care about climate change? We don't want to lower CO2 for its own sake, or for the planet not to get warmer for its own sake, but because it will make the lives of those who live on the planet potentially much worse, even causing the end of some lives.

Consider a couple of different examples of altruistic impact from different points on the political spectrum.

Say you are a progressive who thinks that underprivileged children should have access to a better education. Why do you think this? You could make an abstract argument like "inequality is bad" or "education is good in and of itself," but I'd expect you also have some theory of change that says something like, "If children get a better education, they will get better grades, learn more material, and be better prepared for the job market, ultimately getting better pay than they otherwise would have. And better pay means better quality of life." So, it comes down to you caring about improving others' quality of life.

Or say you are a conservative who believes in limited government. Why do you think this? Again, you could cite some abstract notion like "people deserve to be free," but I'd expect you have a theory of change that goes something like this: "A large government takes in the hard-earned money of the people and often deploys it in ineffective ways. It would lead to better outcomes if the government got out of the way and let people make their own decisions. By better outcomes, I mean more happiness and thriving for those affected." So, you too care about improving the lives of others.

Finally, say you are a green voter and you think climate change is one of the biggest threats facing humanity. You might make a claim like, "We are destroying the only planet we have," anthropomorphizing the Earth, but I'd bet you think something more specific, like, "If we don't curb the addition of greenhouse gases in the atmosphere, humans and animals will suffer terrible consequences." No surprise: You care about improving the lives of others, too.

Nothing in this book will be political in nature. Different political factions have fought over the notion of "the good" for millennia, and I certainly don't claim to have all of the answers. It's true that some of the answers to these questions depend on your values ("I think all humans are of equal moral value") and some depend on empirical answers (such as whether or not it is empirically true that raising the minimum wage has a net benefit on society).

I am simply making the claim that whatever your political and philosophical beliefs are, you likely think that it matters if a person's life is going better or worse. (And if you don't, well, this book is probably not for you.)

Doing as Much Good as You Can

A further claim I make in this book is that if you are going to do good in the world, you should do as much good as possible with the same resources.

This may seem obvious upon reading, but the market for doing good is surprisingly inefficient, and people rarely consider it in this manner. In fact, many find it initially off-putting to think of doing good in terms of efficiency.

And yet, if your goal is to have impact, then it makes sense for you to make as big an impact as you can for the same cost. Doing anything else would be wasteful. Of course, you may have other goals with your philanthropy, such as making a good impression, giving back to your community, or feeling a sense of fulfillment. However, again, if your goal is to have an impact, then you should logically aim to achieve as much as possible with the same resources.

To see what is at stake, consider the following example from Philosopher Toby Ord (bolding is mine)[6]:

> *"Suppose we have a $40,000 budget, which we can spend as we wish to fight blindness. One thing we could do is to provide guide dogs to blind people in the United States to help them overcome their disability. This costs about $40,000 due to the training required for the dog and its recipient.*
>
> *Another option is to pay for surgeries to reverse the effects of trachoma in Africa. This costs less than $20 per patient cured. There are many other options, but for simplicity, let us just consider these two.*
>
> *We could thus use our entire budget to provide a single guide dog, helping one person overcome the challenges of blindness, or we could use it to cure more than 2,000 people of blindness.* **If we think that people have equal moral value, then the second option is more than 2,000 times better than the first. Put another way, the first option squanders about 99.95% of the value that we could have produced.***"*

This isn't merely a theoretical exercise. Even at the highest levels, large philanthropists are not giving nearly as effectively as they could. Consider Jeff Bezos and MacKenzie Scott. According to a 2023 Forbes article[7],

> "Last year, Bezos gave away $122.2 million and has pledged around $12.8 billion in charitable donations, according to The Chronicle of Philanthropy. His mother, Jacklyn Bezos, and her husband Miguel, gifted $710 million to the Seattle-based Fred Hutchinson Cancer Center in 2022."

I won't argue the points here, but here are some questions to consider when deciding whether or not Bezos' mother made a good decision when donating to the cancer center:

- Is this the best organization to consider if she wants to make a donation to fight cancer?
  - Does the Fred Hutchinson Cancer Center have such a large funding gap? In other words, can they utilize the extra funding effectively?
  - Are the types of cancers they work on at the Center the most pressing—those that affect the most people, that are most harmful, or that seem most solvable and aren't being worked on by others?
- Ultimately, fighting cancer is a way of helping people live longer, more thriving lives. If that is the goal, is giving to a cancer center the most effective way to do that?

And regarding Scott, according to a 2023 AP story[8]:

> "The San Francisco Community Land Trust received a $20 million gift, which they first announced in August and which represents about ten times their annual budget. Saki Bailey, its executive director, said that the wealth created in Silicon Valley has created deep inequality, in part seen through the astronomical cost of land and housing."

It is not my goal to disparage anyone's giving—in fact, I believe (and data support this) that most nonprofits are a net good in the world. The question, though, is not whether or not a particular nonprofit does good, but how *much* good it does. Because if you could have done *more* good with the same resources, then you left something on the table.

The Benefactor is not the Recipient, or the Principal-Agent Problem

Imagine your smartphone broke and you have $500 to spend on a new one. How would you go about choosing it? If you are like most people, you'd compare different phones of the top brands, looking for ones that have the features you need at the best price point. That is, you'd try to find the best bang for your buck. It is the rational way to shop as a self-interested person.

Can you imagine closing your eyes and putting your hand into a pile of all the smartphones that exist, maybe pulling out the 1,000th best one, and paying $500 for it, regardless of how well it suits your needs? Obviously, that would be silly.

And yet, when donating to a charity, this is exactly what many of us do. A charity representative approaches us on the street, for example, and asks us for a donation—and we make one, thinking we have done some good. And probably we have. But was it the 1,000th best charity? And why didn't we try to seek out the best donation opportunity we could have, to the extent that doing so is possible?

I think one major reason for this is what I call "the Benefactor is Not the Recipient" problem, similar to the principal-agent problem, which in economics describes a conflict of interest between the owner of an asset and the agent to whom control of the asset has been delegated. When you buy a smartphone, you are the recipient of the purchase, so you have a strong incentive to maximize the impact of your purchase. After all, *you* lose out if you don't! In the case of donations, you are not the recipient at all—these are conferred (or foisted) upon someone you will likely never meet. Whether the benefits of your donation are small, life-changing, or even negative (some organizations do have a negative impact) isn't what's at the forefront of your decision, as it's done without a strong incentive.

ITN Framework

Often, when discussing my work with others, I explain that I strive to have the greatest impact in areas where I can do the most good with my limited resources. A savvy listener will often throw back at me, "Well, how do you measure 'the most good'?" or "How do you know you are doing *the most* good?" These are great questions, and I don't pretend to have the final answers, but I do believe there are some tools and heuristics you can apply to increase the magnitude of your impact.

The main framework I like to use when assessing impact is the **ITN (Importance, Tractability, and Neglectedness) Framework**. Let's go through each term to get a better understanding of its meaning:

- **Importance:** The bigger a problem is—that is, the more people it affects—the more important it is. For example, 39 million people worldwide had HIV in 2022[9], and 18.1 million people worldwide had cancer in 2020[10]. So, according to importance, HIV in 2022 would be more important than cancer in 2020 since it affects more people.[11]

- **Tractability** refers to our ability to solve a problem. Perpetual motion would be wonderful because it would provide us with infinite energy for free, but it is unfortunately not at all tractable. Scientists since the Middle Ages, including prominent figures like Leonardo da Vinci, have worked on designing and building machines that didn't result in net-negative energy—until the laws of thermodynamics were discovered, which showed the endeavor to be a physical impossibility. So even though free energy is a huge problem to solve (and thus *important*), the route to solving it is *intractable*, and pursuing it has resulted in wasted effort that could have been better utilized elsewhere.

- **Neglectedness** gets at how many others are looking to solve the problem. The fewer other resources are allocated toward it, the more likely it is, all else being equal, that your efforts will have an outsized impact. Imagine you are a child on an Easter Egg hunt in your small garden, and 50 eggs are hidden throughout the property. If you wanted to personally get the most eggs possible, which version of the hunt would you be more excited to play?
    - You are the only child looking for eggs.
    - Fifty other children are also looking for the eggs.

With 50 other children looking for eggs as well, your efforts will likely result in you getting one egg on average, whereas if you were the only child looking, you could scoop up all 50 with little extra effort. Even better, if you find all 50 alone, the other 49 children would be freed up to visit other gardens and collect 50 eggs each, resulting in 50 times as many eggs found.

Thus, the more *important* and *neglected* the problem, and the more *tractable* the solution, the more impact you'll likely have by addressing the problem.

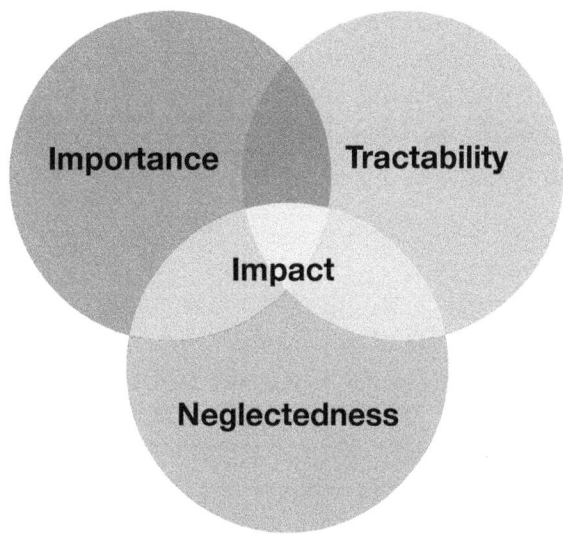

The most impactful opportunities lie at the intersection of Important, Tractable yet Neglected Problems.

Neglectedness is neglected

Having been in this field of work for a while now, I can tell you that although this framework is quite easy to grasp, it is, in practice, hard for many people to integrate neglectedness into their decision-making.

Example 1: Take the case of someone choosing to be a medical doctor in the U.S. Such people likely know that such a job is important in the sense that everyone needs medical care and tractable in that the skills they will gain in medical school can be used to solve the problem. But I would guess that most do not think about neglectedness by asking themselves, "How much would *I* be contributing to lowering the disease burden of the U.S. if I work in this field?"

A naive calculation would be to ask something like, "How many lives have I saved over my time as a doctor?" A more honest calculation of the impact would include in any calculation the question, "What would have happened if I hadn't become a doctor?" And the honest answer to this question is that someone slightly worse than you would have become a doctor in your place, and/or some other doctors in your hospital would have picked up some of your load. Thus, the likely impact of the doctor is much more modest than it initially appears. This isn't meant to disparage doctors—this type of logic can be applied to all professions and shows that it is of the utmost importance for those who want to have an outsized impact to look where no one else is looking.

Example 2: You want to make a very high-impact donation of $10,000. You spend a lot of time researching organizations that offer evidence of their interventions' effectiveness, with solid numbers indicating how much a donation can save a life. You find the organization that can save a life for the smallest amount of money and donate your $10,000 there, satisfied that you did the most good you could.

But you forgot to check if the organization even had a funding gap! If it did not, meaning that it already had sufficient funding for the year, your donation would simply sit in the bank account without being utilized.

Perhaps you checked and found out that the organization had a $10,000 funding gap, which you filled with your donation. Problem solved, right? Well, maybe. If the organization usually fills its funding gaps by the end of the year, you might have only offset another donor who would have certainly swept in and donated at the buzzer. Sure, you freed them up to donate somewhere else, but you don't know where they will donate, and if it is as good as what you would have picked.

As you can see, this can (and does) get complicated, and impact hawks take the complex notion of "neglectedness" quite seriously.

Counterfactuality

A related concept that can help you understand the impact of your work, or really the impact of anything, is something called counterfactuality—the human tendency to create possible alternatives to events that have already occurred.

As in the case of the doctor example above, it is often a very useful question to ask yourself. **What would have happened if I had acted differently?** And it's important to be open to and honest about the answer you arrive at. This can often serve as a clarifying principle for the ultimate impact of some action you could take.

For example, say you see a banner on Wikipedia asking for a donation. You think Wikipedia is a very useful public good and want to support it. Then you remember counterfactuality, and ask yourself: **What would happen if I didn't donate?** Wikipedia has more revenue than expenses year after year, resulting in a growing net asset position. So, if you didn't donate, the answer is very likely that Wikipedia would have slightly less revenue than it otherwise would have, but still have much more than it needs to cover its expenses. And even if expenses outstripped revenues, it is likely that Wikipedia would continue running its fundraiser until others donated to fill the gap you might have filled.

Instead, you decide to donate to the Against Malaria Foundation, a highly effective organization that hands out insecticide-treated bednets to prevent malaria. Why? Because after asking the same counterfactual question—What would happen if I didn't donate?—you realize that your donation will buy a number of bednets that would otherwise not have been bought. Your donation is truly counterfactual, in that the organization would not have had these resources if you hadn't donated.

Counterfactuality can be viewed as a special case of the economic concept of opportunity cost, which refers to the value of the next-best alternative that one forgoes when making a decision.

Marginal Utility

Related concepts I find useful for assessing impact include marginal utility and diminishing marginal utility. To illustrate the concepts, imagine you really like ice cream, and so you buy and eat some. You derive a lot of utility (pleasure) from eating your ice cream. Now imagine you eat a second ice cream—still pretty good and still more utility. Imagine you continue and are on your 45th ice cream. Probably you are much less excited—you're likely experiencing the negative utility of excess and think "Oh God, anything but more ice cream!" This illustrates how each unit of a good you consume can have different utility and how, for many goods, its utility diminishes with each additional unit.

What does this have to do with impact? Well, when you consider giving either your time or your money (your two main options) to organizations that do good, you can consider the marginal utility of your efforts.

If, for example, you are donating $5,000 to an organization that has a $100,000,000 budget, you can likely assume that the marginal utility of your donation will be quite small. The organization likely used the first $99,995,000 to do the low-hanging fruit of their operations and can use the next $5,000 much less efficiently.[12]

If, on the other hand, you donated the first $5,000 to an organization to get it off the ground, it is likely that your donation made a real difference in the operations of that organization and that it will use that first $5,000 to solve what it perceives as the most pressing parts of the problem they are going to solve.

Obviously, there are other considerations to weigh here when assessing marginal utility, but the important point is that at the end of the day, **you want to take the action you calculate to have the highest marginal utility.**[13]

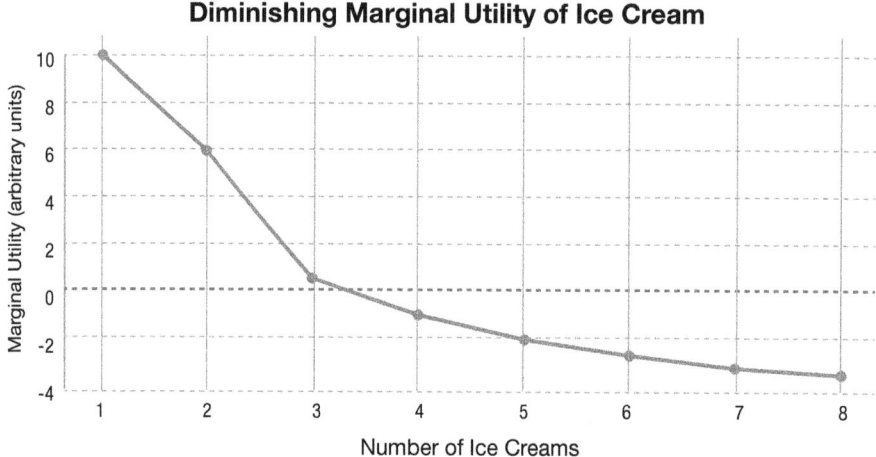

Diminishing Marginal Utility. The first ice cream is great, and the second is also good. The third starts to be enough, and the fourth ice cream and onwards are actually negative: you'd prefer not to eat them because they make you sick! The utility of money doesn't usually dip into the negative, as the next dollar doesn't make you worse off; however, it still diminishes logarithmically in terms of utility.

Note in the above graph that the first donations to a charity have a lot of impact, but each dollar beyond this initial amount buys you less and less impact, indicated by the decreasing values along the impact axis. The charity can use initial donations very effectively, but at some point it can no longer use the next marginal dollar effectively, such as when it has no effective projects to allocate it to or can't find qualified people to hire.

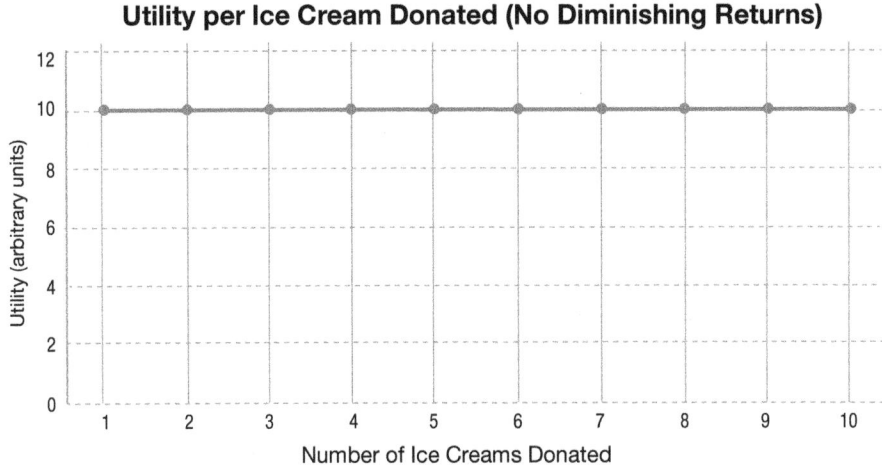

Non-diminishing ice cream example. When you donate ice cream to different people, there is no diminishing utility. Each person gets one ice cream, and they derive 10 utility from it, just as you derived 10 utility from your first ice cream. This means the same amount of resources (the 10 ice creams) can provide way more utility to others than they could if you kept them for yourself.

A Little Bit About Values

I don't want to prescribe values to you. Instead, I want you to work within your value system to identify the most impactful things you can do. I don't believe it is possible to change people's core values very much anyway. Nonetheless, some values motivate my definition of impact that I believe are highly defensible, and I do believe that if I present them to you, there is a chance they will resonate with you, even if you haven't thought about the world exactly in that way before.

Welfare is important

When considering the definition of "positive social impact," we should take seriously the fact that improving the welfare of people—and animals—is a significant component of what we mean by it. Indeed, it might be the only component of what matters, but we don't need to go that far.

Doing more good is better than doing less

This one seems almost tautological, and yet many people don't act as if it's true. It is a mundane observation that, all else being equal, having a more positive impact on the world is better than having a less positive impact.

Impartiality

All people are created equal and, as a consequence, all of their preferences, including welfare, count equally. If I can choose between saving someone in my city or someone 4,000 miles away, all else equal, I should want to save both equally.

Truth-seeking

Most people would say they are truth-seekers, so I don't think the value itself is that debatable. However, in practice, this one is particularly challenging to get right. As humans, we tend to apply frameworks and heuristics to our view of the world, which leads us to develop biases. We want to believe certain things and thus tend to reject narratives that don't fit into our currently accepted frameworks.

But the map is not the territory, and the truth is what it is, irrespective of what we believe. Therefore, it is incumbent upon us to make our best attempt to integrate all the information we receive to form a comprehensive view, even when that necessitates dismissing or modifying frameworks we previously held as absolute. The world is complex, and simple frameworks often fail to meet our needs.

Animals count, too

> *"The question is not, Can they reason? nor, Can they talk? but, Can they suffer?"*
>
> — JEREMY BENTHAM

In this book, I talk a lot about improving outcomes for humans, but anywhere I do, I could also include "animals." I won't go into a deep argument here, but I hope to motivate you enough to continue researching and thinking about the moral status of animals.

So why do animals count? A very condensed version of the argument goes like this:

Many animals feel pain and pleasure. We should not inflict unnecessary[14] pain on any being that can feel it. Therefore, we should not inflict unnecessary pain on animals that can feel it.

Just those two lines include a good argument not to eat meat; we know it is not necessary to live a healthy life, as vegetarianism is associated with a lower risk of health issues than carnivorism[15]. So then the benefit of eating meat is purely pleasure-based. But can that pleasure justify the unnecessary pain and loss of life we inflict on sentient animals who become our meals?

Chapter 2. Causes Worth Fighting For

Now that we are armed with a framework or two for thinking about impact, as well as some values that can motivate our actions, we can start to examine some cause areas more closely that perform well on these frameworks and thus appear, all else being equal, relatively impactful. "Cause area" refers to a broad domain or category of issues that individuals or organizations focus on to maximize positive impact.

Cause Neutrality

If we are maximizing impact, we shouldn't care where we find it, and can thus be **cause-neutral** in our search. Starting off neutral about where the impact comes from, following evidence and reason can lead us to the most effective solutions, wherever they might be. We may feel an emotional pull to donate to something close to our hearts, which is a great instinct. However, if we discover a better opportunity to help even more people, we should consider that instead, even if it is in a totally different area of concern. The people and animals who are being helped don't care what we are passionate about, and we want to help as many of them as possible to the greatest extent we can.

Top Down

If you talk to someone about their donations and ask how it came to be that they donate to a particular charity, you will often hear something like:

> "My relative was diagnosed with X and then I realized it was an important issue and I started giving to X."

Or

> "Someone approached me on the street about cause X, and I signed up to donate to it monthly."

It is great that these people are donating to causes they believe in. However, if their aim is to maximize impact, they might want to take a more holistic, top-down approach to solving the problem, ensuring they aren't leaving anything on the table. Indeed, it would be surprising if a random encounter with someone on the street led you to donate to one of the millions of charities worldwide.

An impact-maximizer will be systematic and rigorous in their decisions about how to give.

Which Cause to Pick? An Approach

You might be convinced that you should maximize your impact, but still not know where exactly, or to what organizations to dedicate your time or money (or both). The following is a quick three-step process for narrowing down the uncertainty and arriving at an answer to the question.

1. Choose a cause area
2. Choose an intervention
3. Choose particular organizations

Choose a cause area

There are many pressing problems you can tackle with your time and money. The first step is to determine which ones are the most important, tractable, and neglected, as per the ITN framework above. Obviously, this is very hard to get exactly right, given all the uncertainties in the world, but you can use sites like 80,000 Hours[16] or Probably Good[17] to help you narrow your search down to a few.

Choose an intervention

Now that you have selected a couple of cause areas, look for interventions in those cause areas that seem particularly promising at solving the particular problem. For example, if you have animal welfare or improving the lives of animals as much as possible on your short list of cause areas, you might want to focus on an intervention that works on corporate campaigns to increase welfare standards across industries. Alternatively, you might like the intervention of developing plant-based alternatives for meat, dairy, and eggs. The goal is the same, but the interventions are very different.

Choose an organization

If you've picked a cause area and an intervention, the last thing to do is to look at the top organizations that carry out the intervention you are interested in. It isn't enough to know an organization is working on an intervention—you want to know they are doing it well! Just as in the private sector, some organizations are run more effectively and have a greater impact than others, even when working towards the same goal.

To do this well, you can look for online information about the organization, chat with funders in the space about how the organization operates, or meet over coffee with employees of the organization. Many cause areas also have one or more organizations specifically focused on evaluating the best or the most promising interventions and organizations doing work in the cause. Some of these will be discussed later in the book.

You can also reach out proactively to volunteer with the organization if they have a need for your skills and time. By volunteering, you can get a behind-the-scenes look at how the organization works, as well as test your personal fit before attempting to commit to a full-time position.

Other constraints

You likely have other constraints, like geographic requirements, a certain skill set, and salary requirements that need to be considered, too. Whatever your particular situation, be mindful of those constraints throughout this process so that you arrive at an answer that best suits your situation and needs.

Don't forget about counterfactuality

To repeat: you should be looking for counterfactual impact. If you land on an organization to support, ask yourself, "What happens if I don't?" and see if that changes the impact that you have control over.

Top Causes

There are many, many different causes you can dedicate your resources to. Here is a list of areas that perform well on the ITN framework, though it's by no means exhaustive. Additionally, simply because a cause area is listed doesn't mean working in it is inherently good; it really depends on the specific intervention and organization you work with within that cause area.

Global health

Global health seeks to address preventable diseases, malnutrition, and health inequities that disproportionately affect low-income populations, particularly in developing regions. Improving global health not only saves lives but also enhances economic productivity by reducing illness-related barriers to work and education. Interventions such as distributing insecticide-treated bed nets or providing vaccinations are known to be highly cost-effective and have demonstrable health outcomes.

Why It's Impactful: The cost-effectiveness of health interventions in low-income countries means that relatively small investments can lead to substantial improvements in quality of life and reductions in mortality.

Top organizations

GiveWell is widely seen as the top evaluator of high-impact charities in global health and development. At the time of this writing, the top, most impactful organizations are:

- **Against Malaria Foundation (AMF)**[18]: Distributes insecticide-treated nets to prevent malaria in some of the world's poorest regions.
- **Malaria Consortium's seasonal malaria chemoprevention program**[19]: Prevents malaria deaths in children under five by providing preventive antimalarial drugs during peak transmission seasons.
- **Helen Keller International's vitamin A supplementation program**[20]: Reduces childhood mortality and illness by providing vitamin A supplements to children in sub-Saharan Africa.
- **New Incentives' immunization program**[21]: Increases childhood vaccination rates by providing conditional cash transfers to incentivize caregivers to immunize their infants.

For an up-to-date list, please visit GiveWell's Top Charity List[22].

Global development

Global development encompasses efforts to reduce poverty, improve education, enhance sanitation, and strengthen infrastructure in low-income regions. Effective global development programs empower individuals, leading to self-sustaining economic growth and increased resilience against poverty traps. Programs like direct cash transfers can have profound, lasting impacts on individuals' ability to thrive.

Why It's Impactful: Addressing structural poverty not only improves individual livelihoods but also contributes to stable economic growth, which can lead to broader social and political improvements.

Top organizations

- **GiveDirectly** delivers unconditional cash transfers directly to extremely poor households using mobile payment technology. Direct cash transfers are often the benchmark for both global development charities and global health charities: if your charity can't prove that it is more effective than just giving people cash (and the vast majority of NGOs can't), then you should just give people money, because it works, has low overhead, and is extremely scalable.[23]

Animal welfare

Animal welfare focuses on reducing the suffering of animals in various settings, particularly in factory farming, where billions[24] of animals experience intense confinement, poor treatment, and extreme suffering. Interventions in this area include advocating for better animal welfare standards, developing alternative proteins, and promoting plant-based diets to reduce reliance on animal agriculture.

Why It's Impactful: Improvements in animal welfare can alleviate suffering for a large number of sentient beings, and reducing the consumption of animal products has environmental and health co-benefits, amplifying the impact of efforts in this area.

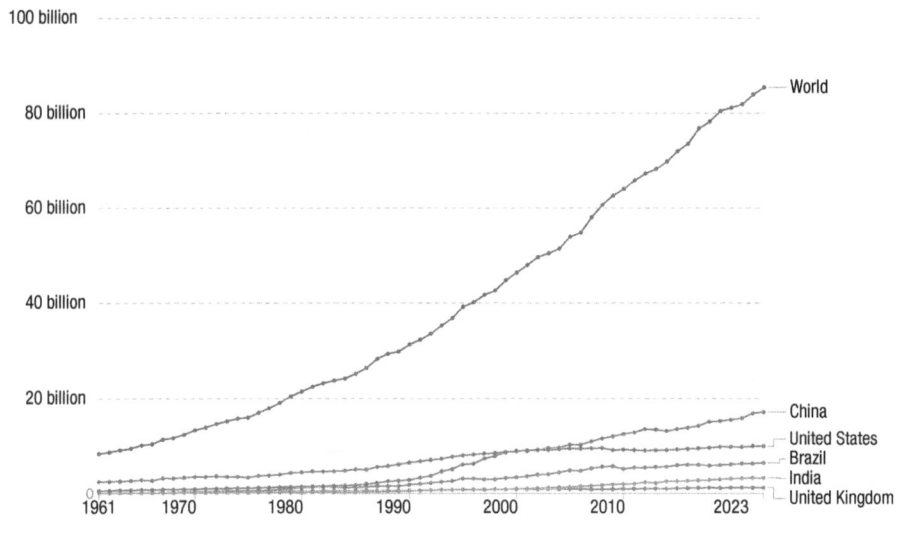

Land animals slaughtered for meat, 1961 to 2023
Based on the country of production, not consumption.

*85 **billion** land animals are slaughtered for meat each year. For fish, estimates are in the **trillions each year**.*

Top organizations

Here are some of the top animal welfare charities recommended in the recent past by the evaluator Animal Charity Evaluators[25]:

- **The Humane League**[26]: Campaigns to reform the way farm animals are treated in the food industry through corporate outreach, public education, and institutional campaigns.

- **The Good Food Institute**[27]: Promotes plant-based and cultivated alternatives to animal products through scientific research, policy initiatives, and market development.
- **Material Innovation Initiative**[28]: Accelerates the development of sustainable and animal-free materials for the fashion, automotive, and home goods industries.
- **Animal Equality**[29]: Conducts investigations and campaigns globally to expose and end cruel practices in animal agriculture.
- **Anima International**[30]: Works across multiple countries to improve the welfare of farmed animals through corporate campaigns, educational programs, and legislative change.

Mental health

Mental health interventions aim to reduce the prevalence and impact of mental health disorders, which are major causes of disability and lost productivity worldwide. Mental health support can include improving access to therapy, developing scalable digital mental health interventions, and community support networks.

Why It's Impactful: Mental health is a high-burden issue often overlooked in public health funding, despite mental illness being one of the leading causes of disability. Effective mental health interventions can restore quality of life and economic productivity to millions, particularly in under-resourced areas.

Top organizations
- **StrongMinds**[31]: Treats depression in women in Africa through evidence-based interpersonal group therapy, delivering measurable improvements in mental health at a cost of approximately $170 per person treated.
- **Action for Happiness**[32]: Provides evidence-based resources and programs to help people take practical action to increase wellbeing and reduce suffering, reaching millions through their courses and community groups worldwide.
- **Vida Plena**[33]: Combines positive psychology interventions with community-based approaches to increase well-being and resilience in Latin American communities experiencing poverty and violence.

For an up-to-date assessment of mental health organizations, consider reviewing the recommendations from the Bloom Wellbeing Fund[34] and Mental Health Funding Circle[35], which conduct ongoing evaluations of organizations in this space.

Biological risk mitigation

Biorisk mitigation focuses on reducing the risk of catastrophic biological events, including pandemics and bioterrorism. It encompasses developing robust health infrastructure, rapid response capabilities, and safe biotechnological practices to prevent, detect, and respond to potential biological threats.

Why It's Impactful: The COVID-19 pandemic has demonstrated how rapidly biorisks can disrupt societies and lead to substantial loss of life. Effective biorisk prevention can save millions of lives and protect global stability by reducing the risk of future pandemics or bioterrorism.

Top organizations
- **Blueprint Biosecurity**[36]: Develops comprehensive policy frameworks to prevent catastrophic biological events, with a focus on strengthening global governance of bioscience and addressing gaps in biosafety oversight.
- **Horizon Institute for Public Service**[37]: Works at the intersection of biosecurity, AI safety, and governance to build capacity among policymakers for navigating complex global risks through research and training programs.
- **SecureBio**: Focuses on preventing biological catastrophes through technical research, policy development, and creating secure infrastructure for high-risk biological research.
- **International Biosecurity and Biosafety Initiative for Science (IBBIS)**[38]: Strengthens the global biosecurity and biosafety ecosystem by developing practical tools, standards, and resources for scientists and institutions working with potentially dangerous biological materials.
- **Nuclear Threat Initiative's Global Biological Policy and Programs**[39]: Reduces catastrophic biological risks through strengthening international biosecurity norms, improving global health security, and developing innovative approaches to biological threat reduction.

For an up-to-date assessment of biosecurity organizations, consider reviewing the recommendations from Founders Pledge[40], which conducts ongoing evaluations of organizations working to reduce global catastrophic biological risks.

Risks from artificial intelligence

Artificial Intelligence (AI) safety and alignment aim to mitigate risks posed by increasingly powerful AI systems, ensuring they are designed and deployed in ways that are safe, aligned with human values, and beneficial to society. This area includes technical research on AI safety, policy work aimed at regulating AI, and efforts to promote ethical AI practices in the development of more powerful and intelligent models.

Why It's Impactful: Advanced AI could bring tremendous benefits but also poses risks that, if left unaddressed, might lead to misaligned systems causing widespread harm or even existential threats. Ensuring the safe development of AI can prevent unintended consequences and preserve human well-being.

Top organizations
- **Center for a New American Security's AI Security Initiative**[41]: Focuses on threat detection and response for advanced AI systems, developing frameworks for identifying and mitigating risks from increasingly powerful AI capabilities.
- **Center for Responsible Innovation**[42]: Works to ensure powerful technologies like AI are developed responsibly with appropriate safeguards, bridging technical research with policy development.
- **Horizon Institute for Public Service**[43]: Builds capacity among policymakers and institutions to address AI risks through research, training programs, and creating pipelines of talent for governance roles.
- **Institute for Law and AI (LawAI)**[44]: Develops legal frameworks and governance approaches for AI systems, with a focus on ensuring advanced AI development remains safe, beneficial, and aligned with human values.
- **Effective Institutions Project's AI Governance Work**[45]: Strengthens institutional capacity to govern AI systems effectively, focusing on improving decision-making processes within organizations responsible for AI development and oversight.
- **FAR AI**[46]: Conducts technical AI safety research focused on alignment, interpretability, and robustness of advanced AI systems to ensure they remain beneficial as capabilities increase.
- **Centre for Long-Term Resilience**[47]: Conducts policy research on extreme risks, including biosecurity and AI safety, engaging directly with governments to improve risk management and resilience.

For an up-to-date assessment of AI safety organizations, consider here, too, reviewing the recommendations from Founders Pledge, which conducts ongoing evaluations of organizations working to ensure that advanced AI systems remain safe and aligned with human values.

Others

Don't feel you're limited to this list! There is good reason to think that these are especially effective organizations, but the movement for effective do-goodery is very young. Uncovering other high-impact cause areas, interventions, and organizations is especially important, as they are likely to be neglected by many looking to do good.

Paths to Impact

Now, for the fun part—actually charting your course to impact! In this section, you'll learn more about different ways to have an impact. For each way, I'll provide resources to help you take the next step.

Individuals looking to make a significant impact often have many paths open to them and can achieve much more impact than it might seem at first glance.

In the abstract, you can think about having an impact in two main ways:

- **Your time**—you spend time working on furthering impactful initiatives
- **Your money**—you give money to impactful initiatives so they can spend their time having impact.

Each of these "resources" you possess can shake out into different ways of having impact. We will cover the major ways in the chapters that follow.

Broadly speaking, unless you are an extremely high earner who donates a large percentage of your salary to top organizations (let's say roughly $100k per year to charity), you'll likely be able to have more impact if you can align your career with impact than you can with your donations, given the sheer number of hours you can work over your career compared to what most earners will be able to donate by comparison. That said, most people can make both impactful career changes *and* meaningful donations, as we'll see later.

Concretely, some common paths to impact are:

- **Your career**—aligning your career with having an impact.

- **Your donations**—donating your excess income or capital to highly impactful organizations.

- **Workplace initiatives**—running impactful initiatives at your organization, such as hosting a fundraising campaign for effective charities, so that you leverage your workplace's resources and capabilities for impact outside of your workplace.

- **Mentorship and Advisory**—mentoring people working at effective organizations to make sure they reach their full potential.

- **Board member**—overseeing an organization to make sure they are steering in an impactful direction.

- **Leveraging your network**—helping connect people to interesting ideas.

- **Leveraging your influence**—spreading ideas of doing good to your network so that more people get involved.

We will go through each of these paths in turn.

Chapter 3. Your Career

Given the tens of thousands of hours most people will spend working, a career is typically their highest-leverage path to creating impact.

> *"Would you tell me, please, which way I ought to go from here?" "That depends a good deal on where you want to get to," said the Cat. "I don't much care where," said Alice. "Then it doesn't matter which way you go," said the Cat.*
>
> — ALICE IN WONDERLAND

Impact Journey Spotlight: The Counterfactual Question

The question that changed **Haindavi Kandarpa's** career was simple: "What would happen if I weren't here?"

Working at BCG on government public health and education projects in India and Bangladesh, she was getting a front-row seat to how policy actually works. But the more she saw, the more frustrated she became. Huge funding allocations from governments and foundations were happening without proper impact measurement. "I could see enormous potential for impact being left on the table," she says.

The work environment made it worse. As a consultant, her job was to execute what clients wanted, not to question whether their approach would actually create change. Even when she knew better solutions existed, the consulting model prioritized client satisfaction over outcomes.

That's when she started asking the counterfactual question that would reshape her career: **"What would be different if I weren't in this role?"** The honest answer was devastating: virtually nothing. Someone equally competent would replace her, and the impact would be pretty much identical.

Growing up in India, where poverty and public health challenges were part of daily life, she'd always felt an emotional connection to this work. But now she was approaching burnout by doing work that *felt meaningful, but was ineffective in practice.*

In her early twenties with savings, no family obligations, and high energy, she realized she had a unique window for taking risks. She created a systematic evaluation of different career paths, weighing impact potential against personal fit and other factors. Charity entrepreneurship ranked highest.

But she didn't feel like a "founder type." She'd internalized stereotypes about entrepreneurs: the loud tech types who "take up space," and that wasn't how she saw herself. Conversations with other founders changed her perspective. "I realized I was overthinking it," she says. "Founding comes in many forms, and the world actually needs people who prioritize evidence and systematic thinking."

That led her to apply to Charity Entrepreneurship's incubation program, a competitive charity startup incubator that launches high-impact organizations to fill critical gaps in the impact ecosystem, complete with seed funding and intensive training.

"I went from feeling replaceable to building something that wouldn't exist without me," she reflects. "The counterfactual impact question didn't just change my career—it became the foundation for how I think about the work itself."

Your Next Step: Honestly assess the counterfactual impact of your current role: what would be different if you weren't there? Then explore paths where your contribution would make a big difference.

For most people, spending their career in a role that has a positive impact is likely to be where they have the most significant impact, given the sheer number of hours they spend in their career. Assuming you work 40 years at 2,000 hours a year, you'll work 80,000 hours in your lifetime. That is a whole lot of time to make the world a better place.

Factor in the neglectedness—the fact that most people don't optimize their career search for having impact—and you'll see that there is a lot of low-hanging fruit for making the world a better place. This is also an extremely rewarding path to impact, as you align your ongoing effort with your values.

On top of this, you are likely still able to donate money to effective charities, so there isn't even necessarily a large trade-off between having impact with your career and with your money.

Making an IMPACT Plan

Like any other major decision you'll make, you'll likely fare better in terms of having impact and being fulfilled if you form a plan of attack when switching careers. This can be broken down into the following steps, starting from personal ideation through to taking concrete steps in the world to get the impactful career you want:

1. **I**dentify your goals
2. **M**ake options
3. **P**rioritize your options
4. **A**djust your options
5. **C**reate your impact plan
6. **T**ackle your impact plan

We will go through each of these in turn. The steps and activities here are a streamlined version of the impact plan framework from High Impact Professionals[49]. The full, free impact plan workbook has a lot more resources than I included in this section, and you can find the link to it in the appendix and the endnotes.

1. Identify your goals

To know what kind of role makes sense for you to jump into, you need to first know what is important to you and what it is you want to achieve. To do that, you need to spend time thinking about this up front. As stated above, you have something like 80,000 hours of work time in your career. Spending even just 5 hours thinking through what is important to you represents .006% of the total hours—a minimal investment!

The exercise has three parts, all outlined below. First, I suggest identifying your top three to five **core values**. These are the values that are most important to you. You can think of your own from scratch, pick from the ones I list below, or use a pre-created list of core values to assist you[50], available with a quick web search or AI prompt. Next, write down your list of strengths that you'll work with to get to impact. Any impactful role you can take will likely leverage your strengths, so it is good to be aware of them. Finally, come up with a brief mission statement[51] for yourself. This statement will be your north star and help you decide what is worth doing and what isn't aligned with your goals.

EXERCISE: Your core values (10 minutes)

Your core values are the principles that guide your decisions and actions. When your career aligns with them, you'll have more motivation and resilience. Review common values (such as Achievement, Compassion, Creativity, Excellence, Fairness, Impact, Integrity, Justice, Learning, Service, Truth), then narrow to your top three to five.

My Top 5 Core Values:

1. _____
2. _____
3. _____
4. _____
5. _____

EXERCISE: Your strengths inventory (10 minutes)

Any impactful role you'll take will likely leverage your strengths: the skills and talents where you naturally excel. List specific strengths (both technical and interpersonal), not general categories, focusing on abilities where others seek your help or where you produce exceptional results.

Example: *Data analysis using Python; Explaining complex ideas simply; Building stakeholder trust; Written communication; Facilitating productive meetings.*

My Key Strengths:

1. _____
2. _____
3. _____
4. _____
5. _____

EXERCISE: Your mission statement (10 minutes)

Your mission statement is your north star. It is a clear description of what you want to achieve and why. Make it specific enough to guide decisions but flexible enough to accommodate different paths, focusing on the impact you want to create rather than a specific role.

Example: *"I will use my technical expertise to help global health organizations make data-driven decisions, ultimately contributing to saving more lives."*

My Mission Statement:

_____

_____

_____

_____

2. Make options

Once you know what is important to you, you can start mapping out some options for your career. Start with the end in mind and then work backward to determine the steps you need to take to achieve it. A good strategy is to consider a cause area that interests you and assess your personal fit with it. Then work backward to determine what you need to do to get in the role.

At this point, you want to be as broad as possible and apply some divergent thinking to generate and explore a large list of paths you could pursue. Don't worry if some seem ridiculous; in fact, the more ridiculous the better. The point is to be creative and comprehensive so you don't miss anything valuable that might come up.

EXERCISE: Generate your options (30 minutes)

Spend 30 minutes brainstorming career paths without filtering or judging. Consider different cause areas (global health, animal welfare, AI safety, etc.), different roles (operations, research, advocacy, etc.), and different organizations (established charities, startups, for-profits). List everything that comes to mind, even the options that feel impractical.

Example: *Climate policy researcher at think tank; Operations manager at animal welfare nonprofit; Earning to give as software engineer; Start AI safety consulting firm; Volunteer coordinator for effective giving organization; Data scientist at global health evaluator; Corporate ESG strategist.*

My Career Options (aim for 10–15):

1. _____

2. _____

3. _____

4. _____

5. _____

6. _____

7. _____

8. _____

9. _____

10. _____

11. _____

12. _____

13. _____

14. _____

15. _____

3. Prioritize your options

Once you have a broad list of options to pursue (some of which can be ridiculous!), you are ready to prioritize. Take the long list of options you generated in the previous step and compare them by making a **weighted factor model**[52] in a spreadsheet. For a simple model, come up with all of the factors that are important to you when choosing your career. Some common factors are:

- (Counterfactual) Impact
- Personal Fit
- Workplace Environment
- Salary

Now, assign weights to the factors. We weigh the factors because they will likely hold different levels of importance in your decision-making. For example, if you believe you are willing to trade off some personal fit for a higher-impact opportunity, you might weigh impact at 0.9 and personal fit at 0.6. So now you might have:

- (Counterfactual) Impact: 0.4
- Personal Fit: 0.4
- Workplace Environment: 0.1
- Salary: 0.1

Once you have identified the factors and assigned weights to them, you can assign scores from 1 to 10 for each factor for each of your career options. Multiply the scores by the weights, and sum up the weighted scores for each career. Sort the spreadsheet, and you can see which career opportunity scores highest according to your own values.

Here is a simplified example:

	Impact (0.4)	Personal Fit (0.4)	Workplace (0.1)	Salary (0.1)	Total
Program Officer at Foundation X	9 (x 0.4)	7 (x 0.4)	10 (x 0.1)	5 (x 0.1)	7.9
Co-founder at new animal welfare charity	10 (x 0.4)	6 (x 0.4)	8 (x 0.1)	3 (x 0.1)	7.5
Researcher at charity evaluator	8 (x 0.4)	4 (x 0.4)	5 (x 0.1)	5 (x 0.1)	5.8

For each option, you score factors 1–10, then multiply by their weights. For example, the first option, the Program Officer role, scores 9 on Impact, resulting in 9 × 0.4 = 3.6. Personal Fit scores 7: 7 × 0.4 = 2.8. Workplace scores 10: 10 × 0.1 = 1.0. Salary scores 5: 5 × 0.1 = 0.5. Add these together: 3.6 + 2.8 + 1.0 + 0.5 = 7.9 total.

This approach may not yield the perfect answer immediately. Your top-ranked option might not quite pass the gut check, for example. If that happens, it usually means one of three things: you misscored something, your weights are off, or you have left out an important factor. One way to test this more formally is the "button test." Imagine pressing a button and instantly finding yourself in the top-ranked role. Really picture it: what you're doing, the impact you're having, and how it feels. If something feels off, dig deeper to understand why. Then go back and update your model with the missing factor. Keep refining until the top option actually *feels* like the top option. You can also run this for your top few choices. Often, they'll be close contenders.

As an example of how this can look in practice, here is an example of a weighted factor model I created a couple of years back, before deciding to go through the Charity Entrepreneurship Incubation Program[53] and start High Impact Professionals.

Job	Job Description	Weighted Value	Intrinsic Motivation	Counterfactual Impact	Career Capital
Charity Entrepreneurship Incubator	This! Could either expand my idea about "Center for Effective Giving" or take on a different meta charity idea (I am most interested in meta charities, as my list here bears out)	7.23	7	7	6
Start a "Center for Effective Giving"	Like Centre for EA, but more based on Effective Giving and "EA Light". Could do this by myself or with CE - there seem to be many benefits with CE.	6.38	7	7	6
NEW CEA Programme Manager	Create and execute new strategy for Community Building Grants for CEA.	6.28	7	7	4
Fund Manager at EA Funds	Fund manager for either the EA Infrastructure fund of the Animal Welfare fund. Part time.	4.63	7	3	4
Effektiv Spenden	Help run Effektiv Spenden (Effective Giving in Berlin). Main projects would be expanding to Switzerland, and spreading GWWC in Germany in conjunction with people @ GWWC. Part time.	5.30	6	6	3
Radical Markets/Blockchain Project	I find blockchain fascinating, both from a technical and economic perspective, and I also believe there is a lot of potential to do outsized good in the world, especially tackling global poverty. I put Radical Markets in the same bucket as I would pursue a project that is the cross-section of both ideas.	5.30	6	4	4

A part of my weighted factor model I built when applying to the Charity Entrepreneurship Incubation Program.

Alternative prioritization exercise: The Five Questions Method

This alternative exercise provides a quick way to prioritize between your options. For a more rigorous analysis, especially if you're deciding between very similar high-stakes options, I recommend using the weighted factor model.

Instructions: For each of your top 3–5 options, answer these five critical questions with a score of 1–5. Add up the scores for each option. Highest total wins. A template is below:

Option: _____

    1. Impact: Would this create significant counterfactual good? (1–5): _____

    2. Fit: Does this match my strengths and energize me? (1–5): _____

    3. Growth: Will I learn valuable skills here? (1–5): _____

    4. Realistic: Can I actually get this role? (1–5): _____

    5. Values: Does this align with my mission statement? (1–5): _____

Total: _____

Option: _____

    1. Impact: Would this create significant counterfactual good? (1–5): _____

    2. Fit: Does this match my strengths and energize me? (1–5): _____

    3. Growth: Will I learn valuable skills here? (1–5): _____

    4. Realistic: Can I actually get this role? (1–5): _____

    5. Values: Does this align with my mission statement? (1–5): _____

Total: _____

Option: _____

    1. Impact: Would this create significant counterfactual good? (1–5):

    2. Fit: Does this match my strengths and energize me? (1–5): _____

    3. Growth: Will I learn valuable skills here? (1–5): _____

    4. Realistic: Can I actually get this role? (1–5): _____

    5. Values: Does this align with my mission statement? (1–5): _____

Total: _____

4. Adjust your options

Your weighted factor model should be revealing. For one, you can now see which options come up on top. You might have one of a couple of feelings:

"Of course! I knew that was going to come out on top! Maybe I even hacked the numbers to get this up there." If you have this feeling, you probably know what you want, so you should just go for it. Some people like this exercise because it reassures them with data that they actually do want what they thought they wanted, and can now remove some other options, or at least be more confident in pressing forward with their top choice.

"What? That can't be right. The thing I really like is way down on the list, and something I don't like is on top." This is also very informative. For one, notice again that you seem to already know what you want, hence your confusion. Second, if something came to the top of the list that you strongly suspect is wrong, you likely have inaccurate weights in your model, or perhaps you are even missing factors that are important to you. Add the missing factors, adjust as needed, and recalculate.

You shouldn't just be guided by your gut here, but don't ignore it either. Once things feel right, proceed to the final step in the process.

EXERCISE: Design quick tests (30 minutes)

Before committing to a major change, you can quickly test your top options to gather real information. Small experiments help you validate your assumptions and adjust the plan without taking big risks. For each of your top two to three options, design a low-cost way to test key assumptions (for example, informational interviews, volunteering 5–10 hours, or creating sample work). Focus on tests you can complete in one to two weeks that give you clear yes/no answers.

Example: *Option: Project manager at global health charity → Test: Email two current program managers requesting 20-minute calls to ask about day-to-day work; volunteer to create one sample program timeline/budget to test if I enjoy the work; assess gut reaction after both.*

My Top Options & Tests:

Option 1: _____

Key assumption to test: _____

How I'll test it (1-2 weeks, clear yes/no answer):

_____

_____

Option 2: _____

Key assumption to test: _____

How I'll test it (1-2 weeks, clear yes/no answer):

_____

_____

5. Create your impact plan

You're almost there! Now you can be fairly confident that the top options you've identified are *really* the top options, so you can move ahead to flesh these out even more. Moving forward with your top options, you can make an ABZ Plan.

The ABZ plan

The ABZ career plan[54] consists of three main elements that will help you maximize your chances of success:

- **One Plan A:** This is the path you are striving for.
- **One or more Plan Bs:** These are paths that are also very promising but aren't your No. 1 option. You'd be happy to do them if A doesn't pan out.
- **One or more Plan Zs:** These are backup plans in case neither your Plan A nor Plan B works out.

Once you have an ABZ plan, make a mini project plan for each of them. Brainstorm and write down the necessary tasks you need to do to make A a reality, as well as a timeline to achieve it by. To help you do this, you can use High Impact Professionals' free impact planning workbook[55].

Make your goals SMART

When you write out your goals for your ABZ plan, or any plan for that matter, make sure they are SMART by making them:

- **Specific:** What will you achieve? What will you do?
- **Measurable:** What data will you use to decide if you've met the goal?
- **Achievable:** Are you sure you can do this? Do you have the right skills and resources?
- **Relevant:** Does the goal align with that of your team or organization? How will the result matter?
- **Timebound:** What is the deadline for accomplishing the goal?

EXERCISE : Create your ABZ plan (30 minutes)

Your ABZ Plan consists of your primary path (Plan A), promising alternatives (Plan B), and a safety net (Plan Z). This framework ensures you're pushing toward your ideal while maintaining flexibility and security. Based on your top options and previous exercises, define your A, B, and Z plans. For each, list 3–5 concrete steps and a realistic timeline.

Example Plan A:

Land operations role at a leading charity evaluator within 12 months. Next steps:

1. Complete the charity evaluator's research training,
2. Volunteer 10 hrs/week for 3 months,
3. Apply to open positions,
4. Network with five current employees.

Make your steps SMART: For each of your plans, especially Plan A, ensure that each step is Specific, Measurable, Achievable, Relevant, and Timebound. For example, instead of "Network with people," you could write "Schedule 3 informational interviews with current employees at target organizations by the end of next month."

My Plan A (Primary Path): _____

Timeline: _____

Next steps:

  1. _____
  2. _____
  3. _____

My Plan B: _____

Timeline: _____

Next steps:

  1. _____
  2. _____
  3. _____

My Plan Z (Safety Net): _____

What triggers Plan Z: _____

6. Tackle your impact plan

Now that you've got your plan, "all" you need is to execute on it. This can be the hardest part, and, if you're like me, you might like to sit in the planning phase as a way to indefinitely put off the doing phase. Needless to say, if you don't do anything, you won't have any impact. Therefore, this step is most critical of all.

The appendix section provides many resources to help you develop your impact plan.

EXERCISE: Your first small step (15 minutes)

The most important thing is to actually start. Break down your path into the smallest possible first step—so small that you have no excuse not to do it—then commit to when you'll complete it. Identify the absolute smallest next action from your Plan A, something that should take no more than 30 minutes to two hours. Schedule it in your calendar right now. Then identify an accountability mechanism.

Example: Email one employee at Foundation XYZ requesting a 15-minute informational call, scheduled for tomorrow at 9 am.

My first small step (must be completable in less than two hours): _____

_____

_____

When I will complete it: _____

My accountability mechanism:

☐ Accountability buddy (name:_____)

☐ Email Devon at hipbook@highimpactprofessionals.org with my commitment

☐ Boss as a Service or similar service

☐ Public commitment on social media

☐ Other _____

Start something new

If you are an entrepreneur, you might want to consider starting a new project of your own, as the counterfactuality on what you are doing is likely very high, since it is unlikely that someone else would have started the project you are starting.

When you accept a job with an employer and you want to have a counterfactual impact, you have to be reasonably confident that you are better than the next best person who would have gotten the job. Otherwise, they could have taken the job and freed you up to do something else. When you start your own project, it is highly unlikely that someone would be as good as you or even that someone would have started a similar project, since it depends on your particular vision and execution.

Starting something new can be net negative, however: for example, if you start a project similar to someone else's and they can do it more effectively, or if you pull donors from more impactful opportunities to yours. If you can't beat the best alternatives out there, you should consider closing shop.

Volunteering

Volunteering with an impactful organization is a great way to utilize your time effectively. Many organizations, even top ones, are in dire need of particular skill-sets that are underrepresented there, either because they 1) are too small to have a dedicated staff with that skill set or 2) because they don't have the pull to get someone amazing.

If you want to start volunteering with an organization, don't go to its site and hope it has a volunteering spot open: it won't. Simply write an email explaining your interest in getting involved. Demonstrate value by showing what you would do to help the organization and why it needs your help. Do the first hour or two of work that you would do if you were actually in your dream role at the organization, and show the leaders there the output. If you are a web designer, for example, mock up different bits of the organization's webpage in a way you believe is more compelling, then email the relevant people at the organization to show off your work and present what the consequences of such a change would be. If you demonstrate value in this way, chances are good the organization will take you on board. You have already demonstrated that you can bring valuable, high-quality work to the table.

Volunteering can also be a great springboard to getting a job with a high-impact organization. The normal application process is that thousands of people apply "cold" (without any personal, "warm" connection to the organization), then the organization has to blindly filter the candidate pool down to one person. Simply due to the numbers, fairly or unfairly, you probably won't pass a certain round, as the organization needs to filter the candidate pool quickly and must apply short-cuts. Your chances are quite low, even if you are exceptional.

On the other hand, if you volunteer even for a short time, demonstrate value, and then pursue a position, chances are good that the organization will take you on board if they have the resources to do so. Organizations want strong talent over anything else, so if you can prove yourself to be strong, you are already leaps and bounds ahead of anonymous people with a cold application and a resume.

If this process is an option, it allows you to test your fit with the organization before going through a lengthy hiring process, taking a chance, and then starting the job only to discover it isn't for you. Both sides win.

Personal fit

This may seem obvious to you, but you should keep personal fit in mind. I often see impact-oriented individuals go all-in on impact while neglecting their own fit, which is a noble but usually naive approach. It's often not only a path to burnout, but it usually isn't even beneficial in terms of impact, as I believe you'll be much more effective and impactful in a role that energizes you and leverages your strengths. There is a trade-off lurking here, so try to strike a good balance between the impact you want to have and the personal fit, but do not neglect personal fit, and don't feel bad if you have to choose it over impact for a job you want. It is the rarest of souls who could give up 100% of personal fit to maximize their impact doing something they don't want to do.

Impact Journey Spotlight: The Full Circle

Simon Ling was in his 50s when he realized his medical career needed to come full circle.

The spark for improving the world had been there since his teens: watching Live Aid coverage of the Ethiopian famine, then taking a gap year to teach in a Kenyan village. Those experiences drove him through medical school and back to Africa for clinical work, nutrition research in Mumbai, and a zinc supplementation study in Bangladesh.

But a chance meeting with an impressive Canadian gastroenterologist changed his trajectory. "You should come to Canada," the doctor suggested. "See what we have there." It was a pivot away from global health toward first-world medicine that would define the next two decades.

Simon thrived in Canada, building a highly successful career in pediatric gastroenterology and rising to division head. The work was meaningful and he excelled at it, but something fundamental was quietly missing. His volunteer telemedicine work with Médecins Sans Frontières, an organization providing medical care in conflict zones and underserved areas, kept his global health passion alive while highlighting stark inequities. Treating a child's severe gastrointestinal hemorrhage via telemedicine in the Democratic Republic of Congo, knowing the same condition would receive millions in treatment resources in Canada, brought those disparities into devastating focus.

COVID brought burnout and a forced reckoning. He stepped down to part-time, creating space for deep introspection he hadn't had in years. "I'd been in healthcare this whole time, but my drive to improve global health had never really been satisfied," he came to realize.

That space led him to discover effective altruism and eventually to High Impact Professionals' Impact Accelerator Program. The coursework and mastermind sessions provided frameworks for major career transitions and connected him with others navigating similar changes.

He did literature review work as a volunteer with Clear Solutions, an organization researching cost-effective global health interventions, which further confirmed his direction. By 2025, he became the executive director of High Impact Medicine, an organization that encourages physicians to direct their skills and resources toward maximum global health impact.

The role represented a return to his original calling, but this time he was armed with two decades of additional clinical expertise, leadership experience, and professional credibility, making him far more effective than he would have been straight out of medical school. And after 15 years of charitable giving, he has just adopted the Giving What We Can Trial Pledge, bringing the same strategic thinking to his charitable giving that he now applies to his career.

Twenty-five years after that pivotal gap year in Kenya, Simon had found his way back to global health, carrying with him everything he'd learned along the way.

Your Next Step: If you've built substantial professional expertise while feeling disconnected from your original purpose, explore how those skills could be redirected toward that original purpose with much greater impact.

Donations vs direct work

If you are truly maximizing impact and open to pursuing an earning-to-give strategy or doing direct work, it is useful to try to model how much money you'd have to donate each year to make it worth pursuing that strategy over just doing the direct work yourself.

I can't provide you with the "right" number, of course, but to try to derive one, you can assess whether the cause area, intervention, or charity you want to support is **funding-constrained** or **talent-constrained.** If it has enough funding, then doing direct work is likely more effective. If there is enough talent available, they probably prefer your money so that they can hire more staff.

In my experience, there is a real market inefficiency in the charitable sector. High-impact roles often go unfilled or are undersubscribed, not because the work

43

isn't compelling, but because talented people systematically undervalue these paths. This creates unusual opportunities for impact-oriented individuals with strong skills.

A quick note about for-profits

Throughout this book, we've been talking about doing good in a non-profit context. Indeed, I think there is a compelling case for this, but maybe not because the non-profit world does good per se, but rather because, unfortunately, not many of the top talent consider non-profit work. Most people enter the private sector and try to maximize their earnings, exploring every opportunity with a profitable business idea. This implies the private market is somewhat "efficient," meaning most low-hanging fruit is likely to have been plucked. If there were a great business idea in the market, a self-interested person is likely to have already tried it.

Contrast that with the non-profit world, where there's a fundamental misalignment: the people paying for charitable work to be done (donors) aren't the same as the people benefiting from the work (end-line recipients of the charity). As long as the charity is appealing to donors, it can stay in business for a long time without ever impacting the world positively. Combined with lower salaries, this means nonprofits consistently struggle to compete for talent. As a result, we can expect many of the best charitable opportunities to still be out there, waiting to be filled by people willing to look beyond private sector compensation.

Nonetheless, I think there is a compelling case to be made for for-profits. First, I'm a big believer that most for-profits create value in the typical "Economics 101" sense: when firms sell products and people buy them, the exchange likely happens because both parties receive value. Thus, looking at a firm's total sales or its market capitalization as a proxy is a good way to know how much value the firm is producing. There are obvious caveats here, and some industries, like tobacco, will cause more harm than good, but for the general things we as consumers choose to buy, both parties gain value.

However, it remains the case that for-profit organizations are generally more efficient at attracting talent. If you don't apply for a particular job, someone else will in your place, and thus, the counterfactual impact of you working there is quite low. With for-profit jobs, it seems particularly important to work in an industry that is net positive and in a role that no one else could have filled.

Another consideration is that working in the for-profit world usually comes with higher salaries, and donations are an effective way to drive impact for most people.

More resources to help you are listed in the appendix.

Getting Started With Career Impact

Your First Steps:

1. **Explore the landscape:** Spend one to two hours browsing high-impact job boards like 80,000 Hours and Probably Good. Don't apply yet—just notice which roles excite you.

2. **Connect with someone on the inside:** Identify three to five organizations that interest you and reach out to one employee at each for a 15-minute informational interview. Ask about their day-to-day work and what skills are most valued.

3. **Test the waters:** Volunteer 5–10 hours with an organization in your target cause area. Create something valuable (analysis, design mock-up, fundraising ideas) to demonstrate your skills while seeing if the work energizes you.

Chapter 4. Your Donations

Donations are an amazing and often underrated path to impact and can be pursued alongside a career shift.

Impact Journey Spotlight: The Intentional Earner

Kim Korte's donation journey started with $10 a month and outrage over $40.

As a student walking across campus 10 years ago, he was approached by the World Wildlife Fund and asked if he would donate. It seemed like a safe choice for his first donation: $10 monthly from his $20/hour job at a cruise holiday referral agency. It felt good to be helping.

Three months later, news broke about the misuse of funds at the WWF. Kim was outraged—not about his $40, but about the principle. His Google search for "how to find good charities" led him to Charity Navigator and Giving What We Can, and "a whole community of people thinking seriously about how to deploy resources effectively," he says.

Kim dove deep into the intellectual foundation of effective giving, consuming Peter Singer's TED talk, Jeffrey Sachs' *The End of Poverty*, Nick Bostrom's *Superintelligence,* and countless blog posts and online resources. This exploration led him to take the Giving What We Can pledge in 2015. "It made rational sense," he says. "I had a lot of moral and philosophical uncertainty, but reducing suffering felt robustly good across many different scenarios."

What started as $10 per month scaled systematically as Kim optimized for greater giving capacity. By 2016, he was donating $30,000 annually. Moving to Berlin for consulting work with Air Berlin, his hourly rate increased, and so did his strategic approach to lifestyle choices. "I was increasingly proud of how much I could donate," he says. He found satisfaction in efficiency, while still enjoying life and spending on things that mattered to him. The optimization enabled him to donate over 50% of his income to areas he cares about while maintaining a comfortable standard of living.

His dedication continued through his role as CTO at the Effective Altruism Foundation, where colleagues discussed veganism with him, quickly convincing him not to eat any animal products. "I noticed my brain fighting the case at first, but the argument was too logical. According to science, at least large mammals probably experience pain in a similar way to us. We want to reduce suffering. So we don't eat animals," he explains.

After automating most of his job away, Kim reassessed what was next, ultimately making a major pivot: switching gears to finance programming specifically to maximize earnings potential for donations. Despite knowing nothing about financial markets initially, he bought textbooks and taught himself how trading systems work, building tools that helped traders make faster, better-informed decisions.

That calculated career change paid off dramatically: Over the subsequent years, Kim donated millions of dollars to organizations working on global health, AI safety, and other high-impact areas. The scale represents thousands of lives saved through his strategic giving, while he continued living comfortably but efficiently.

Now working in IT-security consulting focused on AI safety, the cause he considers humanity's most pressing challenge, Kim has found the ideal alignment. He contributes directly to ensuring advanced AI development goes safely while maintaining a strong salary that enables continued donations. His current role lets him apply his technical expertise to what he sees as civilization's most important problem while continuing to make meaningful donations to impactful causes.

Your Next Step: Calculate what percentage of your income you could comfortably donate if you optimized your lifestyle more for giving, then commit to that amount for one year to test your capacity.

An amazing opportunity

As we've seen before, GiveWell, a well-respected global health and well-being charity evaluator, estimated in 2024 that the lowest cost of saving a life is $3,000, specifically in the context of malaria[56]. They'll be the first ones to tell you the error bars on this estimate are large, but the estimate is nonetheless directionally correct and likely not way off.

This means an astonishing thing: If you donate $3,000 to a top charity at GiveWell, you can actually save someone's life. The cold, hard numbers somehow take the punch out of very important facts like this, but consider a scenario very similar to the one about saving a person who is drowning shared at the start of this book:

> Imagine you are walking down the street in your neighborhood and you see a house on fire. Someone is inside screaming, "Help! Help!" You muster up the courage and do what has to be done: You burst into the house, push through the flames, find the person screaming, and pull them out of the house to safety, both of you breathing heavily, having narrowly escaped death.

Again, if this or something similar were to happen to you, it would be a story you'd remember for your whole life, and, upon your deathbed, would likely be one of your top five most meaningful events.

What $3,000 Can Do

☕	Daily $5 coffee for 2 years	$3,000
🍽	3x monthly $100 dinner for 1 year	$3,000
❤	**Donation - Saves a real human life**	$3,000

Different things you can do with $3,000.

Somehow, thinking about transferring money to a charity doesn't evoke the same emotions, and yet the counterfactual impact is the same. Further, by using money, you don't have to wait to walk by a burning house to have an impact; instead, you can save a life right now. And not just one life: for every $3,000 you donate, another life is saved.

Donating is an incredibly low-hanging opportunity that many people have access to. And of course, you don't need to donate $3,000 to have an impact: If you earn less and have less disposable income, any amount matters. If you can't do $3,000 in one fell swoop, perhaps you can do it over the course of five or 10 years. Even if you donate $100 a year to a top charity, you'll save a life after 30 years. Do what you can!

You are probably much richer than you think

It is easy to compare yourself to those around you and think you are just scraping by, but the reality is you are likely much richer than you think. Check out Giving What We Can's "How Rich Am I?" calculator[57]. If you earn $70,000 post-tax income a year as of writing this, you are in the world's 1% in terms of earnings, and your income is 20.7 times the global median, adjusted for price parity.

Even if you donated 10% of your income to charity, you'd still be in the world's richest 1%.

This bears repeating. After you donate 10% of your earnings, you are still better off than 99% of the world's population. Astounding!

As mentioned, not everyone is in this situation, but my guess is that if you are reading this, you are relatively high up compared to the global median. I recommend that you experiment with the numbers to see how you compare.

EXERCISE: Discover your global wealth position

Most people dramatically underestimate their global wealth position by comparing themselves only to neighbors and colleagues. Let's get the real numbers using the "How Rich Am I?" calculator to see where you actually stand. Go to **givingwhatwecan.org/how-rich-am-i** (or do a web search for "how rich am I calculator") and enter your post-tax household income. The calculator adjusts for purchasing power, so it shows your true position globally. Fill in the results below.

My annual post-tax household income: $_____

I am in the richest_____% of the global population

My income is_____times the global median income

If I donated 10% of my income, I would still be in the richest_____% globally

At 10% giving, I could donate $_____ per year

This would be enough to:

☐ Save _____ lives through GiveWell top charities ($3,000 per life)

☐ Distribute _____ malaria nets through Against Malaria Foundation ($5 per net)

☐ Provide _____ years of income to people living on $2.15/day ($785/year)

Reflection: What surprises you most about these numbers?

_____

_____

_____

What percentage of your income feels achievable to donate this year? _____%

That would equal: $_____ annually, or $_____ monthly

Decreasing marginal utility of money

> *"Nowadays people know the price of everything and the value of nothing."*
>
> — OSCAR WILDE, THE PICTURE OF DORIAN GRAY

Money, like many things, has decreasing marginal utility. Every dollar you get is less useful than the previous one. If you have zero dollars, the first one will allow you to buy some food for the day. If you have one million, the one million and first dollar will allow you to… well, do almost nothing that you couldn't do before.

So it stands to reason that you, a person likely in the 90% or higher in earnings, will create a lot of net good by transferring a dollar from your bank account to that of someone much poorer than you. The dollar hasn't changed, but the value it buys has.

While more money does increase happiness, the effect weakens dramatically as income rises. The happiness boost from your first significant raise when you're earning very little can be substantial: it might mean the difference between struggling to pay rent and having some breathing room. But that same dollar amount added to an already comfortable salary barely moves the needle.[58]

Once your income is already high, the same extra amount of money barely changes your day-to-day experience. You're usually already able to cover needs and many wants, so an identical raise produces only a tiny bump in reported life satisfaction. In fact, to feel as happy as a low-income person does from a modest raise, a high earner would typically need a far larger increase, something closer to adding another full salary rather than just a small top-up.

Giving makes you happier

Not only does research support the idea that earning more has diminishing returns on increasing your life satisfaction, but there is evidence that spending on others promotes more happiness than spending it on yourself. So even if you are "selfishly altruistic," you win.

The seminal study making this case is *Spending Money on Others Promotes Happiness*[59], which shows that individuals who spent money on others reported greater happiness compared to those who spent money on themselves. The research included both correlational and experimental data, enhancing the robustness of the findings. This is consistent with other research[60] that all point in the same direction.

You can even likely complement this with your own experience: Think about the joy you've derived from giving gifts to your family and friends on special occasions compared to the joy you've gotten from similar things you've bought for yourself.

Earning to give

To maximize the effective donating path, some dedicated individuals pursue a strategy called earning to give. Rather than working in an industry with a more direct impact, they pursue high-salary careers, such as those in the finance or tech industries, so that they can donate a substantial amount to charity each year. I know people giving well over 50% of their salary. This strategy is especially valuable for high-earners, as the more you earn, the more you can donate.

Nevertheless, at the time of this writing, I believe it is more important and impactful for people to do direct work rather than pursue this strategy. If you're talented enough to earn hundreds of thousands of dollars a year, you probably have skills that would make a bigger difference working directly for a charity than just donating money. That said, many people have different constraints and niche skill sets, and there are various other reasons why switching careers isn't feasible.

Consider that you might spend $6 on a quick streaming subscription upgrade or a takeout delivery fee. It's small, something most of us barely notice. But that same $6 could buy at least two insecticide-treated malaria nets through the Against Malaria Foundation. Or, consider that 831 million people are living on less than $3.00 a day[61], and a $6 donation could double the income of at least two of them for a day. Imagine how much more value you'd get doubling your income if you were at $3.00 a day compared to the marginal benefit of that premium subscription or delivery fee. These are the kinds of routine, forgettable expenses we could easily redirect to create extraordinary impact.

Tax deductibility

You can make your donations go even further if they are tax-deductible, since you can donate even more money if you go on to get some of it back. But oftentimes, the best opportunities for impact won't be in your country, so donating to them won't give you a tax write-off by default.

Still, there is good news: There are organizations (such as Giving What We Can) in many countries, including the U.S., U.K., and many European countries, that will facilitate your donation, through a re-grant, to the impactful foreign charity in question. Such organizations often also advocate for effective giving, reaching potential new effective donors.

Giving What We Can maintains a list of countries with charities that provide this tax deductibility[62]. Don't see your country in the list? Consider starting a local regranting charity so that your compatriots can also make tax-deductible donations. If you are considering this, reach out to me directly, and I'll try to help out.

Tax deductibility isn't everything

It is essential to note that while tax deductibility enables you to increase your donations, the primary consideration in most instances is the effectiveness of the charity you are donating to. If there isn't a re-granter charity in your country, it makes much more sense to donate to an out-of-country charity that is 100 times more effective than the best charity in your home country—forgoing a tax writeoff rather than donating in-country, way less effectively, just to get a 50% tax writeoff, for example.

Trying the portfolio approach

Some donors may be concerned about risk and want to hedge some of the uncertainties that come with giving. Others may be interested in supporting a variety of causes. Both are good reasons to take a portfolio approach to donations: Dedicating a large portion of your giving, say 80%, to where it does the most good, while dedicating the other 20% to causes you give to for other reasons.

This approach is analogous to diversifying your portfolio of investments to minimize downside risk and hedge your bets; in this case, you can build a donation portfolio that includes charities you support to ease the uncertainties of your other donations, or simply to have fun and get involved with giving to more organizations.

If you want to do the most good with your donations, you will eventually have to confront the fact that the question of where to do the *most* good is an extremely tricky one with many uncertainties involved. This way, you can spread the love to both causes you are passionate about and, for example, to a local institution you feel compelled to support.

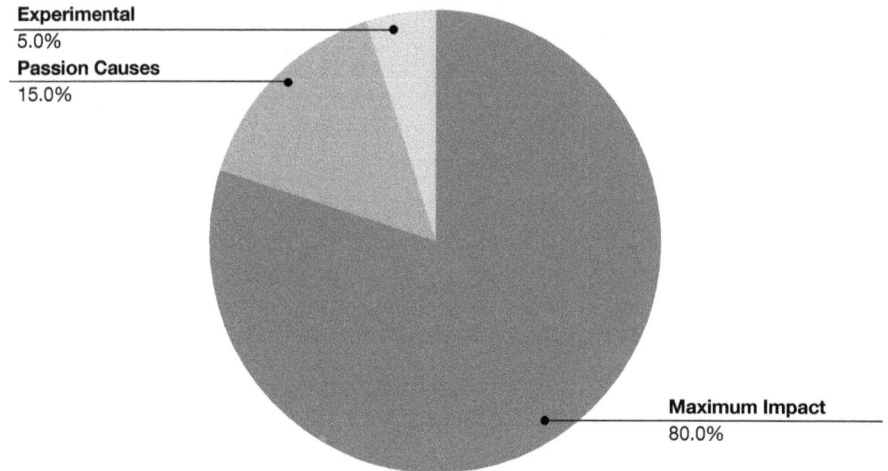

A portfolio approach to giving. To meet your various giving goals, you can create a basket of opportunities to support.

Pledges

There have been numerous pledges for donations that have emerged over the years. These allow you to join a group of like-minded individuals, keep you focused on your goals, and signal your intention to do good.

The 10% pledge

There is a growing community of people (around 10,000 at the time of this writing) who have pledged, through the organization Giving What We Can[63], to donate 10% of their income for the rest of their lives. I am one of them, and it has been one of the most meaningful commitments of my life.

By signing the pledge, you both signal to others that giving is important to you and show that 10% is possible. The organization also offers other pledges, such as the Trial Pledge, which allows you to try out what the pledge feels like by giving a percentage less than 10%. It offers a plethora of other information about effective giving on its website, and I suggest you check it out and consider taking the pledge[64].

Founders Pledge

Founders Pledge[65] is a community of entrepreneurs who have pledged to donate a significant portion of their shares, stock options, or money to charity. In addition to the community, founders have access to advisory services on how to make the most effective use of their donations, as well as financial services to simplify the donation process.

Donate to a fund

Depending on the amount of money you are donating and the time you have to invest in making informed decisions, you may want to consider outsourcing your decision-making to a fund with grantmakers who are experts at identifying high-impact opportunities. As a general rule, the more you donate each year, the more you might want to retain control over your donations. If you donate a relatively small amount, it doesn't make sense to spend a lot of time deciding where to donate, as the overhead of the time is quite large relative to the size of the donation.

Fund managers often have a strong understanding of the space they operate in and will thus likely make better decisions than you would with limited time. They can also coordinate with other actors in the space to make sure the right opportunities are funded to the right amount—in other words, not over- or underfunding opportunities.

Here are some funds you can donate to that focus on maximizing impact. I've broken them out by cause area, so you can first identify what cause area you are interested in and then see the relevant funds.

Global health and development (GH&D)

Fund	Description
Effective Altruism: GH&D[66]	This fund makes smaller grants to newer organizations.
GiveWell: Top Charities[67]	The gold standard in global health and development. These charities have a strong record of great impact and a lot of evidence that they work.
GiveWell: All Grants[68]	Also from GiveWell, but for very promising charities that are still building their evidence base and could turn out to be top charities.
Global Health Funding Circle[69]	A fund run by Ambitious Impact with about 10 individuals, all giving around $100k a year.
Founders Pledge: GH&D Fund[70]	A fund run by Founders Pledge.

Animal welfare

Fund	Description
Effective Altruism: Animal Welfare[71]	This fund makes smaller grants to newer organizations in the animal welfare space.
Animal Charity Evaluators: Recommended Charity Fund[72]	The top charities that Animal Charity Evaluators have identified.
Animal Charity Evaluators: Movement Grants	Makes grants to charities that look promising but are more speculative.
Strategic Animals Funding Circle[73]	A fund run by Ambitious Impact with around 10 individuals, all giving about $100k a year.

Mental health

Fund	Description
Mental Health Funding Circle[74]	A fund run by Ambitious Impact with around 10 individuals, all giving about $100k a year
Bloom Wellbeing Fund[75]	A donor-advised fund focused on improving mental health and well-being in low and middle-income countries. The fund evaluates and supports organizations that deliver evidence-based, scalable mental health interventions.

Climate change

Fund	Description
Founders Pledge: Climate Change Fund[76]	A fund run by Founders Pledge.
Giving Green[77]	Organization Evaluator in the Climate Change space.

Long-term future / existential risk

Fund	Description
Effective Altruism: Long-Term Future Fund[78]	This fund makes smaller grants to newer organizations in the growing field of long-termism.
Emerging Challenges Fund[79]	Fund by Longview Philanthropy.

"Meta" funds

The "meta" option refers to giving to organizations that support the broader ecosystem: in other words, rather than helping recipients directly, they help the helpers. For example, each of the funds listed below is a meta organization. These funds don't deliver services themselves; instead, they identify and support the most effective direct charities. That work is critical—without it, we wouldn't know which organizations are trustworthy or impactful. Because of this, meta charities can be highly leveraged: They can multiply your impact by enabling others to do more good. But like any high-leverage opportunity, there's also more risk: they might (and often do) underperform compared to a well-run direct charity.

Fund	Description
Effective Altruism: EA Infrastructure Fund[80]	This fund makes smaller grants to newer organizations that are Effective Altruism-aligned and support the growing infrastructure of effective philanthropy.
Meta Charity Funding Circle[81]	A fund run by Ambitious Impact with around 10 individuals, all giving about $100k a year.

Cross-cutting

Fund	Description
Charity Entrepreneurship Seed Funding Network[82]	A fund run by Ambitious Impact and composed of a group of donors who seed fund charities that come out of Charity Entrepreneurship's Incubation Program[83], a program that incubates new high-impact charities; this is analogous to seed funding for-profit startups.

"Funging" and additionality

A bit of an advanced topic: it is important to consider **funging** (from the word *fungible*) in the context of your donations if you truly want to have a counterfactual impact.

Even if you've done all the work figuring out the top impactful opportunities with funding gaps, you might want to do some work to determine if these funding gaps would be filled by other donors in the space.

For example, if you donate to fill a funding gap of $50k and another donor would have done so if you had not, you are said to have funged them. This has a couple of implications:

Your donation has no additionality for the grantee. All else being equal, they are going to get the same amount in the world where you don't donate to them as in the world where you do.

Your donation frees up the $50k of the other donor. They can then donate the $50k to another opportunity. If they make better donations than you on average, this is a good thing, as now your target organization gets its funding gap filled, and another great organization that wasn't on your radar will as well. However, if they make less impactful decisions than you, this is a bad thing. You've just freed up $50k that would have gone to a less worthy cause than you would have donated to, so you should have let this donor give to the original opportunity, freeing you up to donate elsewhere.

Forget overhead

When people consider a charity's effectiveness, there is often an impulse to question whether it is misappropriating funds by disproportionately allocating them to administrative purposes, resulting in substantial overhead for the organization with relatively little money reaching end recipients.

But looking at overhead is a red herring. When you are buying a new phone, do you consider how much the company that makes the phone spends on overhead? The thought would never cross your mind. The only thing that matters is that it maximizes the positive impact on your life. Even if the company spent 99% of its funds on overhead, you wouldn't care. So too should it be with the organizations you choose to support with your time and money. You care about what impact you get per dollar, not how much overhead was necessary to get there. Of course, strangely high overhead could indicate that you should take a closer look, but it isn't a problem per se.

Other giving mechanisms

Donor lotteries

The idea behind a donor lottery is to donate along with others into a collective pot of funds. Then, a lottery will take place, with each donor's chances of being chosen weighted by their percent contribution to the pool of funds. The person who is chosen makes a decision on how to donate all of the funds in the pool. In this way, instead of all of the donors having to spend time making decisions about how the money would be most effectively donated, only the winner needs to commit the time. Like a traditional lottery, you have a chance at winning much more than you put in, in this case, granting you influence over more money.

You can find out more about donor lotteries and even take part in one at Giving What We Can's Donor Lottery[84].

Donation swaps

If you want to donate to a charity, but you can't get tax deductibility for the donation in your country, you can try to find someone in another country where there is tax deductibility for the donation, and then try to swap donations with them. In other words, they make a donation to the charity you want, and you make a donation to the charity that they want.

For example, I, a taxpayer in Germany, want to donate to Strong Minds, a high-impact mental health charity, but it doesn't have tax deductibility in Germany. It does, however, have a tax-deductible status in the U.S. Meanwhile, there is a taxpayer in the U.S. who wants to donate to Effektiv Spenden, a regranting organization in Germany, but they can't do that from the U.S. So we both decide we will swap our donations: I'll donate to Effektiv Spenden, and they'll donate to Strong Minds. Then we both get the tax-deductibility in our respective countries.

Set beneficiaries in your investment and savings accounts

In your bank and investment accounts, there is usually a way to set beneficiaries who will receive the designated portion of your assets upon your death. This is a great way to donate, as these designated assets are distributed pre-will, directly to the beneficiaries, so they won't get caught up in an estate where a significant portion of the assets goes to an executor or lawyer.

Bequests in your will

Bequests are provisions in your will that designate the transfer of some assets to a beneficiary, such as an effective charity. There is really no reason not to have a will, as you can set one up quickly to ensure that your affairs are in order should the unthinkable happen. Giving What We Can has a free tool to help you set up a will[85] with bequests.

Donate now or later?

A strategic question that many don't consider is when it makes the most sense to donate to maximize the impact of your donations. There are pros and cons to donating now versus later:

Pros to donating now:
- You know you've done it and won't "value drift"—that is, decide sometime later that you actually don't want to donate.
- The best opportunities could be available now. As more and more philanthropists make effectiveness a cornerstone of their giving, it is plausible that more and more of the low-hanging fruit of impact giving will be plucked, so donating later means you'll get a lower return.
- Helping people now could have positive knock-on effects that you'd forego by giving later.

Pros to donating later:
- The best opportunities for impact could come later. Imagine there is a year when a unique, incredibly impactful funding opportunity comes along, but no one is covering it. If you save up your donations for this time and strike while the iron is hot, you'll have an outsized impact.
- You can invest your money, let it grow, and donate more than you could have if you'd donated the money as soon as possible.
- You can learn more about effective interventions and make better decisions before taking action.
- The world can learn more about effective interventions and uncover even better opportunities before you give.
- You can save money, retire early, and then pursue an impactful career without the need to make money constraining you.

If you are interested in donating when the time is potentially most effective, you can consider Founders Pledge's Patient Philanthropy Fund[86].

Getting Started With Donations

Your First Steps:

1. Make your first effective donation: Set aside a small amount (even $10–$50) and donate it to one of GiveWell's top-rated charities. Experience what it feels like to know your money is having maximum impact.

2. Calculate your giving capacity: Use Giving What We Can's calculator[87] to see where you stand globally and determine what percentage (start with 1–3%) you could comfortably give.

3. Set up a recurring donation: Select an organization that aligns with your values and establish a monthly donation. This builds the habit of giving while supporting organizations with predictable funding.

Chapter 5. Workplace Initiatives

Workplace initiatives are a high-leverage path to impact that most professionals overlook, despite requiring relatively little time commitment.

Impact Journey Spotlight: The Workplace Catalyst

Federico Speziali didn't wait for permission to have impact at work - he created the initiatives he wanted to see.

In 2018, Federico joined a leading Swiss startup and threw himself into the work. The projects were exciting, the team was great, and he was learning a lot. But after two years, he felt the familiar itch to do more good and reduced his workload to focus on how he could make the greatest impact. A pivotal moment was discovering 80,000 Hours, a career guidance organization that helps people find high-impact careers: not because it told him to switch careers, but because it showed him how to maximize impact wherever he was.

He started donating 10% of his income and connecting with Effective Altruism, a community focused on using evidence to do the most good possible. But his real insight was leverage: if he could get more people to join in, it would multiply the impact, and the workplace seemed a perfect place to find leverage.

Federico began experimenting with impact initiatives within the organization. For example, he created an official "Positive Impact" role and organized lunch-and-learns on how to have impact. He tried initiative after initiative, some of which didn't work as planned, but each one established him as someone who could turn ideas into action.

But his breakthrough experiment was a donation drive centered around bonus season. If colleagues were already thinking about unexpected money, why not channel some toward effective giving? The timing was perfect.

Instead of asking HR for permission, he just did it. He found allies among colleagues to help organize the event and connected with a senior leader, who was passionate about environmental initiatives and became a key enabler of the event. By working directly with sympathetic leaders rather than going through formal channels, he moved quickly and got enthusiastic support.

The first event was a major success, raising 25,000 CHF from colleagues. Some were so inspired by the initiative that they donated their entire bonus. Federico systematized the approach, repeating it for multiple years in a row.

His approach was simple: rather than waiting for the perfect opportunity, he learned to just start trying things that seemed promising and see what stuck.

The workplace also became a learning ground for skills he'd later need: building coalitions, communicating complex ideas, and systematically measuring results. After years of proving he could turn ideas into concrete action, he was ready for the next step and left his position to co-found High Impact Professionals with me.

In fact, Federico's track record of workplace initiatives was a major factor in my decision to co-found with him. Rather than just talking about impact, he had consistently demonstrated the ability to mobilize resources, build coalitions, and deliver measurable results. Many talk of "impact", but Federico walked the walk. This marked the start of his direct impact career, transitioning from driving change within existing organizations to building new ones from scratch.

Today, Federico has built a well-rounded impact approach: working at and donating to high-impact organizations, and drawing on years of experience turning good intentions into concrete results. His workplace experiments proved that sometimes the best preparation for mission-driven work is demonstrating you can create change wherever you happen to be.

Your Next Step: Instead of waiting for your employer to create impact opportunities, design one small initiative you could launch independently, then find allies who could champion it with you.

A great place to have an impact is at work. By engaging others within your organization through initiatives, you can often accomplish much more good than you would by going it alone.

Each workplace is unique, so I encourage you to develop an impact strategy tailored to your specific context. Here are some things I've encountered while speaking with various professionals over the years.

Fundraising campaigns

In many countries, people tend to give charitable donations at a certain time of year. In the U.S., U.K., Germany, among others, this is at the end of the year, around the holidays, and to get a tax write-off before the new year. You can join in on this tradition by running a fundraising campaign at your organization.

I've seen many people successfully lead holiday giving campaigns that drum up donations for effective charities. This is usually done through efforts like giving a presentation on why effective giving matters, as well as offering examples of effective giving opportunities. You can set an ambitious yet realistic goal for giving across the team, department, or organization, and use an email drip campaign to remind employees to submit their donations by the end of the year.

You can also create simpler versions of this, such as setting up a giving campaign at Giving What We Can and linking to it in a company Slack or equivalent.

In fact, my co-founder at High Impact Professionals did this and, over the course of two years, was able to raise around $30,000 in addition to his own donations. That is a significant return (resulting in approximately 10 lives saved!) for minimal effort, all because he had the proactivity and courage to present this to his colleagues. Courage may not even be required: employers love people who take initiative and run these positive campaigns.

It is worth noting that you don't need to do this around the holidays. Any time is fair game, and some other times might make even more sense. For example, at High Impact Professionals, we helped startups run fundraising campaigns around so-called liquidity events, where employees with equity would get distributions at the same time. All of a sudden, many employees had a lot of disposable cash they didn't necessarily reckon on, so it was a great time to get them thinking about donating.

Take advantage of donation matching

A surprisingly large number of organizations will match a donation you make up to a certain amount, effectively doubling your donation potential. You can search the web for organizations that match donations or ask your HR department if your organization offers a donation matching program.

I had one case where someone worked for the London office of an international organization. He was aware that the U.S. office had donation matching but the U.K. one didn't, and so lobbied to get it added to the U.K. benefits, as well. If there isn't currently a donation matching program at your organization, try to get it added to the menu!

Pre-tax deductions of donations through payroll

Some employers also allow you to make donations pre-tax, so it comes off the top of your salary. This reduces your effective income, resulting in lower taxes on your salary and allowing you to donate more than you otherwise could have. Check with your HR department to see if you have this benefit. If you don't, ask how you can get it implemented at the company.

Volunteer time off

Many organizations allow employees to take a certain number of service days each year, during which they volunteer at a nonprofit of their choice and give back to the community. People tend to do hands-on things like volunteering at a soup kitchen. While admirable, it is likely that you can do a lot more good by trying to figure out if your specialization is needed by effective charities. For example, if you are a data scientist, you could identify some charities you find to be exceptionally effective and write to them proposing how you could do some data science work to give them insights into their work or help them become more efficient.

Plant-based lunches

If your workplace provides lunch or snacks, you can contact the operations department and request that they offer only vegetarian or vegan options to minimize animal suffering.

Do your core business in a more socially impactful way

Depending on your core business and your personal remit, you can often steer your organization in a more socially impactful direction to help you have some impact on the job. As an example, one consultant I worked with pitched a VC client on investing in a cellular agriculture startup, which was creating real meat but without any of the animal suffering and with less CO_2 emissions. This was a double win: The financial upside for the client was large, as was the social impact.

CSR departments

A big potential source of impact is getting your Corporate Social Responsibility (CSR) department, should you have one, to make donations more effectively, as many control large sums of money. In practice, it can be challenging to influence where the money goes from the outside, and I haven't come across many success stories of doing this effectively. If the company has a large CSR department, it typically has strong views on how the money should be donated—usually to targets that align with the business's mission, which primarily serves the marketing function of the organization.

A better approach is to try to get on the CSR department committee that makes decisions, so that you are directly responsible for choosing where the money is donated. This takes more time and effort, but since most people just want to clock in and out of their jobs, taking the initiative and proactively working to get on the committee can potentially be a quick path to influencing a lot of donations.

In general, I think this path is underexplored, and I would be keen on people experimenting and reporting back to the community what works and what doesn't, so we can benefit from the learnings.

Workplace group

Instead of going it alone, you can join forces with other like-minded individuals within your organization and create a group that spearheads these initiatives. This has many benefits:

- There is strength in numbers.
- You have someone to hold you accountable.
- If someone is absent, there is someone else to pick up the slack.
- You can accomplish more.

These groups can then run any of the initiatives you've read about here, or come up with their own. You can also join an existing workplace group.

Summary

As we've seen, there are many different ways to have an impact at your organization. Running an initiative requires some proactivity and openness to push things forward, but nothing magical. We've explored various approaches here, and I hope you've found something viable for your organization that excites you. However, I also encourage you to consider your specific context and develop a tailored plan. And remember, we've only scratched the surface: There are likely thousands of different approaches one can take to making an impact on the job.

Some people I've spoken to are hesitant to run these initiatives out of fear of putting themselves out there; some were even wary of posting a link to a donation page in their Slack. While understandable, I think these fears are misplaced. These requests are quite small, and people have an easy way to say no; if they say no, nothing bad will happen. In addition, employers typically appreciate employees who take initiative and contribute culture and value to their organizations, so this will likely be viewed more as a feather in your cap than something undesirable. And finally, think back to the example of saving someone's life by pulling them out of a burning building. You can likely save many lives by running one of these initiatives, and the courage you need is much less than running into a burning building! So please do what you can.

Please let me know about any initiatives you end up running, so I can include them in future versions of this playbook.

EXERCISE: Identify your workplace allies (15 minutes)

The first step to running successful workplace initiatives is identifying colleagues who might be receptive to effective giving ideas. Think about who's already shown interest in charitable causes, who asks thoughtful questions, and who has influence in your organization.

List three colleagues who might be interested in effective giving. For each, note why they might be receptive and draft a simple pitch tailored to what motivates them.

Example: *Colleague: Sarah (Engineering Lead) Why receptive: Volunteers at food bank, always analyzes decisions with data Pitch: "I've been getting into researching the most effective charities and found some that are a really great deal. I know you are interested in volunteering, so I thought you'd like to hear more. Want to grab lunch sometime this week and chat?*

My Workplace Allies:

Colleague 1: _____

Why they might be receptive:

My 2-sentence pitch: _____

_____

Colleague 2: _____

Why they might be receptive:

My 2-sentence pitch: _____

_____

Colleague 3: _____

Why they might be receptive:

My 2-sentence pitch: _____

_____

Getting Started With Workplace Initiatives

Your First Steps:

- **Test the waters**: Share one article about effective giving or a high-impact cause in your workplace Slack, Teams, or email list to gauge interest.
- **Find allies**: Identify two to three colleagues who might be interested in impact and invite them for coffee to discuss starting a workplace initiative.
- **Launch a micro-campaign**: Start small with a specific, time-limited campaign (like a holiday giving drive to a specific charity) rather than trying to establish an ongoing program immediately.

Chapter 6. Trusteeship

Trustee roles offer exceptional leverage for impact and are in high demand, yet rarely appear on impact-oriented professionals' radars.

Impact Journey Spotlight: The Unexpected Expert

Luciana Vilar thought she had nothing to offer nonprofit boards. "These organizations are full of PhD researchers and policy experts," she assumed. "What could a corporate finance person possibly contribute?"

After years of corporate work across Switzerland, Australia, and the Netherlands—constantly searching for meaningful impact—Luciana had built the exact skills that mission-driven organizations desperately lack. When she joined the boards of Happier Lives Institute and Condor Initiative through connections from High Impact Professionals, she discovered she was often the only person in the room with significant finance experience.

"They needed someone who could create proper budgets, think strategically about funding pipelines, and translate research for corporate audiences," she explains. At Happier Lives Institute, her corporate perspective helps position wellbeing research in ways that businesses are more apt to use. At Condor Initiative, focused on AI safety in the Global South, she brings financial rigor to an area where technical expertise often overshadows business fundamentals.

But her trustee work is just one part of a broader impact strategy. In her day job, Luciana spent three years methodically building what would become her corporation's ESG office, working from within to embed social and environmental considerations into core business strategy. She had to navigate corporate politics, build coalitions across departments, and craft compelling business cases for why sustainability mattered to the bottom line. Today, as Head of Sustainability Partnerships, she's reshaping how a multinational corporation thinks about its impact beyond profit.

"Over the past eight years of learning about effective altruism and crafting my impact path, I've come to conclude that transforming big corporations is one of my biggest opportunities for impact," she reflects. "You need to build to a position of power to actually move the needle." Her strategic approach to building that power, such as spending years establishing credibility and climbing to her current position as Head of Sustainability Partnerships, exemplifies the long-term thinking required for corporate transformation. In addition, Luciana also donates 10% of her income, including to some of the organizations where she serves as a board member, ensuring her financial support aligns with her strategic contributions.

Luciana's approach shows the power of patience and strategic positioning. Rather than abandoning corporate work for traditional nonprofit roles, she's built influence where it can create change while simultaneously strengthening mission-driven organizations from the outside. Her journey proves that impact doesn't always require choosing sides; sometimes, it requires building bridges.

Your Next Step: List three professional skills you take for granted, then research which high-impact organizations might desperately need exactly those capabilities.

A role that is critical to a healthy nonprofit and yet is not on many impact-focused people's radars is that of the non-profit trustee.

A trustee is a person ultimately accountable for a nonprofit organization in much the same way as a board member of a for-profit company. In nonprofits, trustees can also bear the title of a board member. While not generally involved in the day-to-day operations of the nonprofit, a trustee is often called upon for significant decisions that the organization needs to make, as well as for budget review and approval. Perhaps the most significant role of a trustee is overseeing the CEO or executive director and holding them accountable, potentially even removing them from their position if necessary. The trustees are ultimately accountable for the organization, so they play a critical role. While the specifics vary by jurisdiction, trustees typically carry one or more of several core responsibilities:

- **Fiduciary duty:** Ensuring the organization's financial health and that its resources are used appropriately for the mission.
- **Strategic oversight:** Setting and monitoring progress toward organizational goals and strategy.
- **Legal compliance:** Ensuring the organization meets all regulatory requirements and operates within its legal mandate.

- **Risk management:** Identifying and mitigating organizational risks, from financial to reputational.
- **Executive oversight:** Hiring, evaluating, supporting, and, when necessary, replacing the executive director or CEO.
- **Fundraising support:** Often contributing financially and helping open doors to funding opportunities.
- **Mission stewardship:** Ensuring the organization stays true to its mission and serves its intended beneficiaries.

At a minimum, a trustee will need to attend a couple of board meetings a year and vote on various agenda items, such as approving the budget. But that is only the minimum. A strong board member can take on more active roles and be like a senior, though unpaid, employee on the team.

Many organizations are in need of good board members, and this is a high-leverage role. You can often commit the amount of time you want, as the organization is likely to be happy with any time you can provide if you have skills and expertise they lack. That said, it is a serious commitment, so whatever time you offer, you should ensure you can deliver.

If you have particular charities in mind that you'd like to support as a trustee, you can visit their websites and send them a message indicating your interest in joining the board. Don't worry if there is no role posted for it.

There are many services where you can find organizations looking for board members. For example, the EA Good Governance Project[88] is effectively oriented and allows you to sign up as a potential board member for organizations to see your profile and reach out accordingly.

Getting Started As A Trustee

Your First Steps:
- **Honestly assess your skills**: Write down three to five specific skills or experiences you have that would benefit a non-profit board (financial expertise, legal knowledge, marketing skills, etc.).
- **Research smaller organizations**: Look for early-stage, high-impact organizations that match your skills and cause interests. These often have a greater need for trustees than established organizations.
- **Make direct contact**: Reach out to the executive director or current board chair at two to three organizations, clearly explaining the value you could bring as a board member and why you care about their work.

EXERCISE: Identify your trustee skills (10 minutes)

High-impact nonprofits need trustees with practical business skills, but many board members come from academic or research backgrounds. Your professional expertise is likely more valuable than you think.

List your top five professional skills that you've developed over your career. Focus on practical capabilities that small organizations (under 20 staff) typically lack, such as financial planning, legal expertise, HR systems, marketing strategy, fundraising, operations, or technical skills.

Example: *1. Financial modeling and budgeting (15 years in corporate finance) 2. Risk management and compliance (managed regulatory audits) 3. Hiring and talent development (built teams from 5 to 50 people) 4. Fundraising and donor relations (raised $2M for university program) 5. Strategic planning facilitation (led 10+ strategic planning processes).*

My Top 5 Trustee Skills:

1. _____

(Years of experience: _____)

2. _____

(Years of experience: _____)

3. _____

(Years of experience: _____)

4. _____

(Years of experience: _____)

5. _____

(Years of experience: _____)

Which of these skills do you suspect is rare in nonprofit boards?

_____

Which skill could I provide the most value with in 2-4 hours per month?

_____

Chapter 7. Mentoring and Advisory

Mentoring and advising are exceptional options for experienced professionals who want flexible, high-leverage impact by helping others reach their full impact potential.

Impact Journey Spotlight: The Talent Multiplier

Samie Dorgham realized that helping talented people reach their potential might be more impactful than any direct work he could do himself.

His path started with confronting frustration: Public sector projects across manufacturing, pharma, and retail felt bureaucratic and "one step removed from real impact." The long hours without visible change led to burnout, during which he discovered 80,000 Hours, a career guidance organization focused on high-impact careers.

This discovery led him to AI startups working on COVID-19 impact measurement and healthcare patient experience, which was much more directly meaningful work. But the 2022 tech layoffs sparked a different insight: what if his biggest contribution wasn't his own work, but helping others optimize theirs?

The coaching that had helped him recover from burnout revealed his potential for a similar impact on others. Through the High Impact Professionals' Impact Accelerator Program, he tested this hypothesis systematically, using mastermind sessions to refine his approach before piloting free sessions with impact-oriented professionals. The program's experimental mindset proved essential, giving him 6 to 12 months to test ideas, fail quickly, and scale what worked.

"If I can help talented people at high-impact organizations become the best versions of themselves, that multiplies impact far beyond what I could achieve individually," he says he realized. When clients insisted on paying after just two sessions, he knew he'd found his leverage point.

Now scaling with best-in-class certifications, he focuses primarily on people who want to maximize their impact while remaining open to others who could benefit. His business model reinforces the impact of multiplication: He's maintained his 10% giving pledge for five years, with clients knowing that a tenth of their payments go to support effective charities.

Combined with money coaching (helping people build the financial foundations necessary for taking career risks) and technical work for his parents' publishing company, Samie has created a practice that multiplies impact at multiple levels while honoring his personal values. The money coaching component directly addresses the financial runway issue that prevents many talented people from making impactful transitions.

His own journey taught him that creating the time and space to explore new directions is crucial for anyone considering a major career shift. "You can't figure out your next move while you're still overwhelmed by your current situation," he explains. "The breakthrough comes when you give yourself permission to step back and experiment."

This philosophy underpins much of Samie's work. "I don't just help people with career transitions," he explains. "I help them understand how their specific talents could create the most good in the world, while building the practical foundations to make those transitions possible."

Your Next Step: Identify one skill or insight that has been transformative in your own life, then explore whether sharing that knowledge could multiply impact through helping others optimize their contributions.

A great option for those with more professional work experience is mentoring or advising either charities or individuals who are in a particularly impactful role. As I've learned by running the High Impact Professionals' Impact Accelerator Program, this is not on most professionals' radars. But after hearing about it, many decide that this will be a relatively easy way for them to have an impact. Not only that, it's a role that many experienced professionals are suited for and can find time for, as the commitment is flexible.

If you are looking to change careers, advising and mentoring others can also provide insight into how charities operate, giving you an insider's view before committing to a switch.

In the best cases, you can really help people and organizations remove roadblocks that would have taken them much longer without you (if they ever would have found the solution at all), so this can be extremely high-leverage.

Advising a charity

Many charities have an advisory board, which is just what it sounds like: a group of people who advise the charity on various issues. These roles are usually unpaid, and unlike a trustee, an advisor is not accountable to the organization in any way. In fact, there is no formal legal relationship at all.

An advisor can guide the charity through any issue it needs help with:

- Strategy
- Accounting
- Legal work
- Risk management
- Finance

So, if you have a particular area of expertise, chances are you would be invaluable to a charity that doesn't already have this type of support.

Advising isn't the only thing advisors do, however. They also lend credibility and reputation to a charity. Charities, therefore, bring on advisors who are high-profile, even if they don't advise the charity more directly. If you have a relatively high profile and a strong reputation, you may be a good candidate.

To get started advising charities, identify those that you think are particularly impactful. Then simply write them and explain you'd like to get involved and what you have to offer. Many charities would be excited to get such an offer and are in need of advice in key business areas. To help you identify charities that would be a good fit, try to determine the level of your skills and reach out to charities that are smaller, as they'll likely have a greater need. For example, Oxfam is massive and unlikely in need of legal advice, but a two-person startup charity probably doesn't have a legal team at its service. Have some calls with the charities you identify, and you'll get a feel for what they need.

Mentoring an individual

In addition to advising a charity, you can also mentor a promising individual who needs it more directly. Many small charities lack strong or established hierarchies, so not everyone has a supervisor to learn from, especially in areas where an employee's performance needs improvement.

If you are an experienced professional, you can provide this mentoring and help out with an individual's particular bottleneck. This can be in any one of the following areas:

- A particular specialization. For example, a junior Python programmer is the only tech person at the organization and thus has no boss. You help her improve her coding, as you are a specialist in software engineering.
- Standard business practices. You might help a co-founder make a one-year plan and set OKRs to achieve their goals; you help them prioritize their work and give them direction when you think they are steering the wrong way.
- Coaching. For an employee who is frustrated with their boss, you act as a life coach, provide emotional support, help identify solutions, and build up agency and proactivity in the employee.
- Some combination of the above, depending on your strengths.

Take an honest assessment of yourself and your strengths to determine where you have the greatest leverage to help others.

Once you know where you can help, you can reach out directly to high-impact charities you've identified as ones you think could most benefit from your support. Most will be happy to receive your message, and if they think they wouldn't benefit from your support, they will let you know, so it is not costly on either side to take the first step by contacting them.

EXERCISE: Create your advice menu (10 minutes)

Organizations and individuals need specific help, not just vague offers to "chat sometime." An advice menu clarifies exactly what value you can provide in a focused conversation.

List three to five topic areas where you could provide immediate, actionable advice in a single one-hour conversation. Keep topics broad enough that multiple people could benefit from the help.

Example: *1. Financial planning and budgeting; 2. Career transitions from corporate to nonprofit; 3. Team management and leadership; 4. Fundraising strategy; 5. Operations and scaling*

My Advice Menu:

1. _____

2. _____

3. _____

4. _____

5. _____

Which topic could I help someone with TODAY if they called?

_____

General tips

Here are some tips that apply to both advising a charity and mentoring an individual:

Make the expectations of the relationship clear from the outset. Define clearly what type of support you want to give, how often, and for how long. Whatever you commit to, follow through.

Start small and then increase commitment. In your dating life, you wouldn't plan an eight-hour first date. So too in advising. Start small with brief calls and no promises to gauge the situation and allow both parties to determine if they are getting value. At the end of the call, assess how it went and decide what your next commitment is.

Know you'll likely hit diminishing returns. Depending on the type of relationship you have, you'll likely hit diminishing returns in terms of "wisdom" you impart on your advisees. The first 5 to 10 hours are likely gold, as in this time you can communicate the map to the part of the maze that you've seen, but others may not have. After this, expect each subsequent call to be potentially slightly less valuable. At some point, you should have a feeling for whether future calls would be worthwhile or if you've said all that you have to say. This isn't always true, especially if the nature of your help is more general, such as life coaching, or in dynamically changing situations. In these cases, you can always take a fresh look at a new situation and try to get your client from A to B.

Don't be afraid to say you don't know. Be straightforward with what you know and what you don't know. If you don't know something, think of someone you know who does and offer to connect your advisee with them. You aren't here to be impressive; you are here to help someone have an impact.

Getting Started With Mentoring and Advisory

Your First Steps:

Identify your expertise niche: Specify exactly what knowledge or skills you can offer (e.g., "digital marketing for nonprofits," not just "marketing").

Start with a single organization: Reach out to one small, high-impact organization working in a cause you care about, offering one or two hours of specific help on a defined problem.

Structure a pilot engagement: Propose a short trial (two to three sessions) with clear deliverables, allowing both parties to assess the fit before committing to ongoing mentorship.

Chapter 8. Leveraging Your Network & Influence

Leveraging your network is perhaps the highest return-on-time path to impact, requiring minimal effort while potentially catalyzing major career changes or donations from others.

Impact Journey Spotlight: Building What's Missing

Daniel Wernstedt doesn't wait for impact opportunities to appear; he creates them by identifying unmet needs and building solutions.

Since 2017, when he discovered effective altruism as a consultant, he's been entrepreneurial about impact. Beyond his yearly donations of 10% of his salary, he's had his hand in dozens of impactful initiatives: running career coaching clubs in Stockholm, facilitating impact cause area discussion groups, running book clubs, speaking about impact at corporate events, organizing social gatherings, and board service with Effective Altruism Sweden and Ge Effektivt, a Swedish effective giving organization. His philosophy: "Have agency, start small, push ideas forward, don't get stuck in analysis paralysis."

A large opportunity came from recognizing a market failure. Skilled professionals in his network wanted to contribute to important causes but couldn't find efficient ways to help. Meanwhile, high-impact organizations desperately needed senior expertise but were too funding-constrained to afford it, making access to experienced consultants who could provide strategic advice a major win they otherwise couldn't afford.

Daniel created the missing market through Agile for Good, which was launched after his "world improvement" session at a Nordic agile conference that inspired and attracted 50 professionals. He designed a comprehensive system of one-hour problem-solving sessions during lunch breaks, in which senior professionals could immediately demonstrate their expertise to high-impact organizations. But the key innovation was his role as bridge-builder: Daniel conducts pro-bono intake calls with organizations in need of support to better attract the relevant competencies among the professionals in his Agile for Good network, which sets up both sides for success. This preparation means the one-hour sessions deliver immediate value, with professionals showing their worth right away and organizations getting genuine solutions to real problems. The structure helps mitigate the typical frustrations that kill pro-bono relationships before they start.

The opportunity he created now serves more than 150 volunteers across 25-plus organizations, with 85% of participating professionals agreeing to commit more pro-bono time to doing good. "I realized there was enormous untapped potential waiting for the right structure," he explains.

Now working for Ge Effektivt, Daniel continues expanding access to impact opportunities. His "Make it Count" events in Stockholm reflect his organization's broader mission to make the impact movement more accessible beyond traditional demographics. These quarterly gatherings combine brief effectiveness presentations with social connection, together raising more than $9,400 in lifetime donations while building a bigger tent for people interested in strategic giving and impactful careers.

Daniel's approach shows that impactful careers can be built by identifying gaps and taking the initiative to systematically fill them. Through persistent experimentation across multiple channels, he's created a lasting infrastructure that multiplies impact far beyond his individual contributions.

"Get involved in small things and think creatively," he advises. "The worst outcome is doing nothing when you see problems that could be solved."

Your Next Step: Identify one unmet need you've noticed where skilled people want to help but can't find appropriate opportunities, then take initiative to create that missing connection point.

Perhaps the best way to have an impact per unit of time is to leverage your network and, relatedly, your influence, especially if your network is large and diverse. If a high-impact organization is looking to make a key hire and you reach out to your network and ping the top five people who'd be a great fit, and one gets the job, you probably committed at most one hour to the endeavor and yet had an extremely large impact, as without you the organization would have had a worse person in the role.

Leveraging your network and acting as a connector is relatively straightforward. Still, you need to consider it and be willing to do it for a significant enough return on investment, even if you have competing priorities.

The three levels of network leverage

If anyone comes to you with a need, such as "Can you help me with skill X? I need some advice," you can respond at the following three levels:

Level 1

A junior approach is to ask yourself, "Can I help?" If the answer is no, simply say 'no'. Don't say you'll help if you can't, even out of a sense of duty or pride. If the answer's yes, then you say yes and proceed to help.

Level 2

You consider all the people you know who might be able to fulfill the request. This requires proactively thinking about the request broadly and understanding the goal. Then you can reach out to the appropriate people you know and make intros accordingly.

Level 3

You consider all the people you know who might know someone who could fulfill the request. For example, someone may need legal help with U.K. law. You don't know any U.K. lawyers, but you are good friends with a banker in the City of London, and you decide to reach out to him to ask him about lawyers he knows. Note that if he does this too, as does everyone after him in the chain, you are virtually guaranteed to find a connection. You are often just two hops away from someone who can help.

Note that you can do all of these steps even if you can fulfill the original request yourself. It may be the case that someone else is better suited than you to help, either because their skills are superior, they are less time-constrained, or for other reasons. Don't be afraid to protect your time, but always aim to add value if you can and it isn't too costly to do so.

Make proactive connections

In addition to handling inbound requests, you can proactively connect people in your network with high-impact opportunities. People in your network can do any of the things outlined in this book, from donating money to effective causes to switching careers to a high-impact organization.

Over time, you will develop a sense of what different people in your network have to offer and are looking to do, and then you can connect them with the resources they need—and don't forget to think of this in the higher levels as described above!

By leveraging your network, you can use your influence to help shift minds and hearts toward a more impact-oriented perspective. Instead of making a connection between a person in your network and a resource they'd benefit from, this is about you talking about what is important to you and sharing ideas you think are solid. This is particularly effective if you are well-known and influential, though everyone has a circle of influence through which they can spread their ideas.

Post on social media

Posting on social media about your beliefs about impact and efficiency in doing good creates a conversation around these topics and puts them in the arena where they can be held up against other ideas. Even if you have a small following, people will likely see and react to your posts, even if they don't hit the "Like" button. Standing up for what you believe in publicly gives you a stance that other people have to contend with and shows others what is important to you.

Friends and family

You can also spread the things you care about with friends and family. While you might be concerned about being too pushy, there is obviously a legitimate line you can stay within to share views that are important to you, all in the hopes that others will hear the ideas and take them forward.

Professional network

As outlined in the Workplace Initiatives section, the general idea is to leverage your organizational trust and political capital to share impactful ideas and run workplace initiatives that further these ends.

EXERCISE: Map your network for impact (15 minutes)

Your network contains untapped potential for impact. These are the people with skills, resources, or influence who simply haven't encountered the right opportunities yet. By mapping who you know and what they could offer, you can become a high-leverage connector.

List 10 people you know well and note each person's unique resources, expertise, or influence. Then identify one specific way you could connect them to impact opportunities based on what they have to offer.

Examples: *1. Jamie (data scientist, loves problem-solving) → Connect to charity evaluator needing statistical analysis 2. Robert (wealthy, values education) → Share GiveWell's work on cost-effective education programs. 3. Lisa (marketing executive, cares about animals) → Introduce to animal welfare org needing brand strategy. 4. Tom (early-career consultant, exploring careers) → Send 80,000 Hours career guide.*

My Network Map:

    1. Name: _____

    Their resources/expertise:

    _____

    How to connect them to impact:

    _____

    2. Name: _____

    Their resources/expertise:

    _____

    How to connect them to impact:

    _____

    3. Name: _____

    Their resources/expertise:

    _____

    How to connect them to impact:

    _____

(continue for a total of 10 connections in your network)

Fundraisers for special events

One effective way to leverage your influence is by running a social media fundraiser for a significant life event, like a birthday. I've seen many people easily raise $1,000-plus by simply posting a campaign a few weeks before their birthday, saying that, instead of presents, they'd like you to consider donating to a high-impact opportunity.

And you don't have to just limit this to birthdays. Be creative. You can host a fundraiser for a wedding, a long-distance bikeride, a marathon, or any other special event you want to celebrate.

Sometimes you can create your own "event." I've seen people just say they are going to put up, for example, $2,000 that will go toward matching the first $2,000 of donations their post generates. Again, be creative.

If you are interested, you can set up a fundraiser with Giving What We Can[89].

In general, the more you concentrate on sharing your views and living your ideals, the more you'll likely influence those around you to jump on board.

Getting Started With Influence

Your First Steps:
- **Map your network's potential:** Spend 30 minutes listing 10 people in your network whose skills or resources might be valuable to high-impact causes.
- **Make one introduction:** Connect one person in your network with a high-impact opportunity that genuinely fits their interests and skills.
- **Create a personal fundraiser:** Set up a small birthday or special event fundraiser for a high-impact charity, with a modest goal that your immediate circle could help you reach.

Chapter 9. Take the Next Step

As I said at the start of this book, I want you to take action as a result of having read the book, not just idly absorb knowledge.

Combine, Combine

I want to explicitly state this obvious fact: the impact paths we've discussed are not mutually exclusive, meaning that you can successfully do more than one simultaneously. Anything that takes your time will trade off on other things that take your time, of course, but you should investigate your goals and determine what mix of approaches is right for you. As you learn more and things change, you can also revisit your choices.

Decide Which Paths to Take

At a high level, you'll want to decide which combinations of actions make the most sense for you. You may want to prioritize one that you estimate will lead to the most impact, or the one you are most likely to get started on. The details will depend on you.

A helpful tool here is the High Impact Professionals' Impact Plan Workbook[90]. That workbook is based on the one used in High Impact Professionals' Impact Accelerator Program, which helps experienced professionals take action toward high-impact careers through six weeks of facilitated cohort discussions, a global network, and career frameworks. To date, the Impact Accelerator Program has facilitated numerous high-impact career transitions.

Stay on Track with Different Accountability Mechanisms

While personal productivity is outside the scope of this book, I have seen many people struggle with procrastination, and I believe it is worth addressing here. My goal is to help you make progress toward your goals.

Find the next small step

To increase the odds of your success, break down your path into the most minuscule steps, ensuring none are too trivial to exclude. The next step in finding a job might be simply scheduling a phone call with an employee at an organization that you are interested in. With donations, it might start with you giving $100 to a worthy cause. By making the first step small, you lower the bar to doing it and thus increase the chance you'll continue to follow through.

I encourage you to find an accountability buddy with whom you can periodically check in to deliver updates. This can be a friend who will hold you to account for what you've promised to do. You can check in with them daily or weekly and report what you intend to do during the timeframe—and then check back in to say whether or not you accomplished it. If you don't want to bug your friends, you can do this with a service like Boss as a Service[91], of course, at a price.

Take a Mini-Pledge Right Now

In case I wasn't clear: I really, really want you to take action and let nothing get in your way!

To that end, I ask you to **write down one thing you will do within the next seven days after reading this section.** Email me[92] your pledge. I'll read it.

Quick-Shot Advice for Different Barriers

One more set of points before you get going. For a long time now, through working with professionals on having more impact, I've seen many of the same barriers come up over and over again. If you are struggling to move forward, try the tips here to take the next step. If you don't know why you are finding it hard to take the next step, you can investigate what comes up when you read each of the following to see if something resonates with you.

Most of these apply to career switches, but could also apply to any other path.

"I'm so overwhelmed and paralyzed by too many options."

Makes sense! A lot of people experience this. Especially if you are trying to maximize your impact rather than merely make it a bit bigger, you've taken on a gargantuan task. Because that implies there is just one correct answer and that everything else is suboptimal.

While technically true, you can't know what your best-in-the-world option is in the real world, where you have limited time to figure it out.

Instead of sitting there paralyzed, try to:

- Recognize that spending time thinking and not acting can be suboptimal if it continues for too long. Consider this a cost to your approach.
- Reduce complexity in your decision as much as possible by setting additional constraints to limit the problem's size. If you are too unbounded (able to work anywhere in the world, in any cause area, for any amount of money), you'll never be able to narrow things down.

- Work through a program like High Impact Professionals' Impact Accelerator Program. We've worked with hundreds of people and helped them figure out and pursue their impact goals, even after suffering from analysis paralysis.
- Timebox your process—and promise yourself you will stick to it.

"I'm not good enough to make the switch."

There are two possibilities here:

1. **You have imposter syndrome.** I see this one happening so much! Many smart, talented people come into the same room and talk to each other, and each one believes the others to be more worthy of being there than themselves. If this is the case, you need to tackle your imposter syndrome. There are many reliable online sources that provide guidance on how to do this.

2. **You are actually not good enough.** First, don't rule out that you have imposter syndrome, as if you do, you will probably first think, "I don't have imposter syndrome, and I really am not good enough." However, if you are fairly certain that something is missing, first identify what it is. Do you not have the skills you need to succeed? Are you not motivated by the work? Once you figure out what is going on, either decide that you'd be better suited for a different role or get better, skill up, and then apply for the role again.

"I'm scared to make the switch."

Totally normal! Change is hard!

An important yet simple question I ask people who are scared to switch is this: "If you change careers and after a year decide it isn't for you, could you get your old job back?" The answer, way more often than not, is an easy yes. If you are a good employee, employers will want to keep you. Once people realize this, the barrier is much lower because they know they aren't foreclosing on an option, and this makes things less risky.

You should also meditate on the nature of status quo bias, which causes humans to strongly prefer maintaining the current state of affairs rather than moving to a new situation. One way to combat status quo bias that works for me is to pretend you are starting with a blank slate and could start everything anew. You have no job and no constraints. How could you craft your career going forward? Would you choose the current role you are in? For most people, this perspective helps them see clearly that, no, they would not, in fact, choose the role they are in again, and therefore see many new possibilities about how to move forward.

I should also mention that not every feeling is a bias and that sometimes fear serves a strong and relevant role in our lives, even if it is often misplaced in the modern world. So try to assess if you are afraid of something "real" (such as questioning your ability to feed your kids if you go down a certain route) with fears that seem overblown upon reflection ("Gosh, this would be a big change for me!")

"I'm just not pushing things forward."

I hear you. This is me a lot of the time. Procrastination is tough.

This reason is a bit vague, so it would be helpful to try to hone in on what is going on.

- First, check the basics and nail them:
- Are you sleeping well?
- Are you eating well?
- Are you exercising?

Form hypotheses about what is going on and test them using principles from Cognitive Behavioral Therapy (CBT). This means identifying the specific thoughts that are holding you back, questioning whether they're really true, and testing alternative perspectives. For example, if you think "I'll fail at this career switch," ask yourself: What evidence supports this? What evidence contradicts it? What would I tell a friend having this thought? Don't make things big and scary, but approach them more like scientific experiments. Get introspective and curious.

Even if you can't identify what needs correcting (humans are complicated!), you can still attempt to make behavioral changes. Check out the procrastination section for tools you can use to limit distractions. If you struggle with this, you might also be a good fit for High Impact Professionals' Impact Accelerator Program[93].

Most importantly, don't be hard on yourself. Treat yourself as you would a friend who was struggling. Be compassionate.

"I don't have the skills to get a high-impact job."

This is similar to the "not good enough" answer. Either you are right, and you need to up your skills. Or you are wrong, and you have imposter syndrome.

"I don't know which type of job is most impactful."

It is challenging to determine which job is most impactful for several reasons. For one, it is challenging to determine the actual impact of an organization. Figuring out the most impactful role depends not only on which organization is most impactful in absolute terms, but also on where your particular skills and experience are needed the most. In other words, it doesn't help to join an impactful organization where you can't be leveraged.

As a quick first pass, you can go to a job board to find effective positions, like Probably Good[94] or 80,000 Hours[95]. They have already narrowed down the field of all jobs to those that are particularly effective. Of course, you'll want to do your own due diligence to see how the jobs compete in your view, but this is a great way to filter down the field.

You can also sign up for High Impact Professionals' Talent Directory[96], used by 200 high-impact organizations when they are sourcing for talent.

You can also timebox yourself to make an impact plan, as discussed earlier in the book.

"I'm worried about financial stability."

This is a real concern for many people, especially mid-career professionals who have established a particular career track, as they will typically face two financial challenges: one from leaving the field where they've built up their salary, and another from joining the non-profit sector.

I don't have much to say here because if the numbers don't work for you, they don't work. But there are a couple of things I'll mention.

One is that it is highly likely to have a great life with less salary than you'd expect. Check out the earlier section on personal income and wealth. If you are reading this, it is likely that you are significantly wealthier than the vast majority of the world's population.

I often see that something like ego is also at play. Our society affords a high status with a salary, so lowering the salary implies a corresponding lowering in status, which is unfortunate. As a result, people often struggle psychologically with the idea that they may be perceived as having a lower status if they switch from a for-profit to a non-profit organization. I can remember these thoughts going through my head when I made the plunge about a decade ago. I think it is important to meditate on this and really try to decouple salary from status. This, combined with believing the fact that you can likely live a great life with a bit less, could get you over the line.

On the other side of the coin are people who, in my view, go too far. I know many altruistic people, for example, who take a paltry salary on purpose and don't do things like get insurance or pay into their pensions because they are keenly aware that any money that they save could instead be going, right now, to someone desperately in need, and they can't justify that. While their altruism is admirable, I fear they may go too far and will at least partially regret their decision later, especially should something happen that causes them to rely on some rainy-day savings, like an unexpected unemployment or health issue.

"I feel like the problems are too big and my contribution won't matter."

I have felt this many times before, so I get it. Sometimes it can feel as if the weight of the world is so much to bear that you should rather let yourself be crushed down by it than try to hold it up. After all, 600,000 children die of malaria each year. What does it matter if you donate $10,000 to the Against Malaria Foundation and save two of them?

And yet it does matter. For it isn't the percentage of the problem you solve that is important, it is the absolute amount of good you do. You probably recognized that when you read the above about how saving two lives is worth it, even if there are billions more to save. Indeed, saving two lives is an amazing act. Those are two lives, like those of your children, your spouse, your parents, your siblings. Two people who can go on to lead happy and fulfilling lives who otherwise would have died.

This is also true when you find out that people are doing much more good than you are, for example, if they are donating orders of magnitude more than you. You might think it impossible, but I talked to an earning-to-give individual who donates $200,000, about half his salary, who had low feelings of self-esteem and felt he was doing nothing because he knows billionaires are donating much more. You can experience this feeling all the way up the impact scale, so it is crucial to maintain perspective and recognize that every bit of good done counts.

"I don't know anyone in the space."

It is never too late to build out your network. I've found people in the effective giving community to be among the most helpful individuals I've ever encountered. Many people working in the space will be more than happy to have a call with you and to help answer questions or connect you to others who could help you. And although many of these individuals are altruistic, there is also a significant incentive: as described in Leveraging Your Network, those seeking impact view it as high value to connect you with the right person. By spending 30 minutes talking to you and understanding your needs, they can potentially facilitate a connection that might not have happened otherwise. That is counterfactual impact right there.

Something else

Do you have a barrier that prevents you from having more impact and is not listed here? Please reach out and tell me about it! I'd like this list to be as comprehensive and helpful as possible.

Chapter 10. Final Thoughts

Now that you've made it this far, you've hopefully gotten a much clearer sense of what a high-impact path could look like for you. We've covered a lot of ground together, from understanding what impact truly means to exploring the most pressing causes worth fighting for, to mapping out concrete paths you can take, starting today.

The journey to impact isn't always straightforward. As we've seen, there are frameworks like ITN to help you evaluate where your efforts will go furthest. There are complex questions of counterfactuality to consider, as well as questions about where you are best positioned to make a difference.

But here's what I hope you've taken away. **Having impact—real, significant impact—is actually within your reach.** Whether that's through donating effectively (remember, $3,000 can save a life), shifting your career to directly address the world's most pressing problems, mentoring others to amplify their impact, or simply using your existing workplace as a platform for change, you have more power than you might think.

And you don't have to choose just one path. As we've discussed, the most effective impact-driven professionals often blend multiple approaches. You might maintain your current career while donating strategically. You might volunteer your specialized skills while advocating for workplace initiatives. You might serve as a trustee while leveraging your network to connect others to opportunities they wouldn't otherwise find.

If you're feeling intimidated by the scale of the world's problems, remember what we discussed: It's not about the percentage of the problem you solve, but the absolute good you accomplish. Those two lives you save by donating $6,000 to a top GiveWell charity? They're real people with families, hopes, and futures that wouldn't exist without your action. The hundreds of animals spared suffering through your advocacy? They feel pain and relief just as intensely as we do.

I've been on this journey for over a decade now, and I can tell you from experience that aligning your life with impact isn't just good for the world. It is also deeply fulfilling. There's something profoundly energizing about waking up each day knowing that your work genuinely matters, that you're using your limited time on this planet to make it meaningfully better for others.

So what now? I hope you'll take that micro-step we talked about. **Write down one action you'll take in the next seven days.** Email it to me at hipbook@highimpactprofessionals.org. I meant what I said at the beginning of this book: I really do want you to take action, not just consume information.

Perhaps that action marks your first strategic donation. Maybe it's reaching out to someone working at an organization you admire. Perhaps it's about bringing up effective giving in your workplace's Slack channel. Whatever it is, make it concrete, make it specific, and make it happen.

The world has enough people who care in principle but never quite get around to acting. What the world's billions of people and trillions of animals need is for you to care enough to do something about it.

You now have the knowledge. You have the frameworks. You have the resources. The only question left is, what will you do with them?

I believe you can do extraordinary good. Prove me right.

Appendix

Resources

Paths to impact

Here are some resources that I hope will help you on your journey:

- Resources from High Impact Professionals:
  www.highimpactprofessionals.org/
- Impact Accelerator Program
  www.highimpactprofessionals.org/impact-accelerator-program
- Impact Plan Workbook—A six-part workbook designed to guide you in finding your most impactful options and the next steps to pursue the
  tinyurl.com/impact-plan
- Talent Directory
  www.highimpactprofessionals.org/td-job-seekers

More resources available here:

- Programs by Ambitious Impact (AIM):
  www.ambitiousimpact.com
- Charity Entrepreneurship's Incubation Program—A cost-covered training program that gives a small cohort of talented people from all over the world everything they need to launch a field-leading charity
  www.charityentrepreneurship.com
  www.charityentrepreneurship.com/incubation-program
- Founding to Give—launch a high-growth company to donate to high-impact charities
  www.aimfoundingtogive.com
- Research—Designed to equip participants with the tools and skills needed to identify, compare, and recommend the most effective charities and interventions
  www.aimresearchprogram.com
- Probably Good
  probablygood.org
- 80,000 hours Job Board
  jobs.80000hours.org
- 80,000 Hours Career Guide
  80000hours.org/career-guide/

Donations
- Take a donation pledge as part of the High Impact Professionals' Pledge Club
  www.givingwhatwecan.org/pledge/hip

General information & resources from Giving What We Can:
- Donation pledge information
  www.givingwhatwecan.org/pledge
- Giving Guides
  www.givingwhatwecan.org/guides-and-resources
- Other resources
  www.givingwhatwecan.org/get-involved/videos-books-and-essays
- High-Impact Charities to Donate to
  www.givingwhatwecan.org/best-charities-to-donate-to-2025
- Tax-Deductible Regranting Organizations for different Countries
  www.givingwhatwecan.org/get-involved/tax-deductibility

Workplace initiatives
- High Impact Professionals resources
  www.highimpactprofessionals.org
- Fundraising campaigns overview and step-by-step guide
  www.highimpactprofessionals.org/corporate-fundraising
- Key Factors for Success in Organizing a Fundraising Campaign at Your Company
  www.highimpactprofessionals.org/post/key-factors-for-success-in-organizing-a-fundraising-campaign-at-your-company
- More information on many of the themes discussed in this book section, including links to multiple webinar recordings
  www.highimpactprofessionals.org/post/expanding-your-impact-effective-giving-beyond-donations
- Giving What We Can
  www.givingwhatwecan.org
- Numerous resources on effective giving to support your fundraising campaigns, workplace/professional group, and other efforts, including Giving Guides
  www.givingwhatwecan.org/get-involved/videos-books-and-essays
  www.givingwhatwecan.org/guides-and-resources
- Get support for creating and hosting a fundraiser.
  www.givingwhatwecan.org/fundraisers

- Request a Giving What We Can workshop/talk on hosting an effective giving effort at your workplace or community group.
  tinyurl.com/gwwc-talk
- One for the World: Request support with effective giving outreach at your workplace/professional group, or company
  tinyurl.com/eg-support
- Consultants for Impact: Workplace Group Toolkit
  www.consultantsforimpact.org/workplace-groups

Trustee
- EA Good Governance Project
  www.eagoodgovernance.com/
- Article about non-profit boards
  www.cold-takes.com/nonprofit-boards-are-weird-2/

Mentoring and advisory
- Magnify Mentoring: Helps to connect prospective mentors and mentees.
  www.magnifymentoring.org/
- Apply to be a mentor here.
  www.magnifymentoring.org/mentor
- Charity Entrepreneurship Mentorship: Mentor their (newly) incubated charities www.charityentrepreneurship.com/mentorship.
- AIM Founding To Give Mentorship: Mentor (newly) launched high-growth companies formed to donate to high-impact charities.
  tinyurl.com/mentor-aim

Leveraging your network & influence
- Giving What We Can Fundraiser
  www.givingwhatwecan.org/fundraisers

Figures

Page 3: Malaria Deaths by World Region. Adapted from Our World in Data. "Data Page: Malaria deaths by world region", part of the following publication: Esteban Ortiz-Ospina and Max Roser (2016) - "Global Health". Data adapted from IHME, Global Burden of Disease. Retrieved from https://archive.ourworldindata.org/20250909-093708/grapher/malaria-deaths-by-region.html [online resource] (archived on September 9, 2025).

Page 4: Number of poor. Adapted from Our World in Data. World Bank Poverty and Inequality Platform (2025) – with major processing by Our World in Data. "Below $3 a day – World Bank" [dataset]. World Bank Poverty and Inequality Platform, "World Bank Poverty and Inequality Platform (PIP) 20250930_2021, 20250930_2017" [original data].

Page 5: Average Charity vs Top Charity.

Page 11: ITN Framework.

Pages 14 & 15: Marginal Utility of Ice Cream.

Page 21: Land Animals Slaughtered. Adapted from Our World in Data. Food and Agriculture Organization of the United Nations (2025) – processed by Our World in Data. "Number of chickens slaughtered to produce meat" [dataset]. Food and Agriculture Organization of the United Nations, "Production: Crops and livestock products" [original data].

Page 25: Paths to Impact.

Page 49: What $3,000 Can Do.

Page 54: Donations - Portfolio Approach.

All photographs are courtesy of the individuals depicted.

Endnotes

1. GiveWell. "How Much Does It Cost to Save a Life?" GiveWell, April 2024, accessed 18 November 2025, https://www.givewell.org/how-much-does-it-cost-to-save-a-life

2. Our World in Data. "Malaria deaths by world region." Our World in Data, accessed 18 November 2025, https://ourworldindata.org/grapher/global-malaria-deaths-by-world-region.

3. World Bank. Poverty, Prosperity, and Planet. Washington, DC: World Bank, 2024.

4. Roser, Max, and Hannah Ritchie. "Many of us can save a child's life, if we rely on the best data." Our World in Data, 2021, accessed 18 November 2025, https://ourworldindata.org/cost-effectiveness.

5. Effective Altruism. "The Introductory EA Program." Effective Altruism, accessed 18 November 2025. https://www.effectivealtruism.org/courses/introductory-program.

6. Ord, Toby. The Moral Imperative toward Cost-Effectiveness in Global Health. Washington, DC: Center for Global Development, 2013.

7. Liu, Phoebe. "Jeff Bezos Announces He's Donated Nearly $120 Million to Help People without Housing." Forbes, 21 November 2023, accessed 18 November 2025, https://www.forbes.com/sites/phoebeliu/2023/11/21/jeff-bezos-announces-hes-donated-nearly-120-million-to-help-families-experiencing-homelessness/.

8. Associated Press. "Philanthropist MacKenzie Scott reveals the groups that got some of her $2.1 billion in gifts in 2023." AP News, 8 December 2023, accessed 18 November 2025, https://apnews.com/article/mackenzie-scott-donations-962490e92faab36492b7481205ec7249.

9. U.S. Department of Health and Human Services. "Global Statistics." HIV.gov, accessed 18 November 2025, https://www.hiv.gov/hiv-basics/overview/data-and-trends/global-statistics.

10. World Cancer Research Fund. "Worldwide cancer data." World Cancer Research Fund International, 2022, accessed 18 November 2025, https://www.wcrf.org/preventing-cancer/cancer-statistics/worldwide-cancer-data/.

11. For simplicity's sake I am ignoring another important component: the effect sizes of the different disease burdens. And, it goes without saying that both of these problems are important to solve, even if one is currently bigger than the other.

12. Note that this isn't always true: sometimes the marginal utility increases the bigger an organization gets, as it achieves economies of scale. You need to look on a case by case basis.

13. This applies to anything you do in life, not just when considering impact. For example, the next meal you eat should be the one that gives you the highest utility, however you define it.

14. The word "unnecessary" is doing a lot of work here. We could imagine scenarios

where we simply have to inflict pain, or we deem it necessary for some broader goal, such as in the grim case where not inflicting pain would cause even more pain. A mundane example is not making the speed limit 1 mph: we know that if we set it at 45 mph we will cause, in expectation, a certain number of traffic deaths each year, and yet we quite reasonably don't make the speed limit 1 mph to remove them all.

15. Allen, Nicholas B., et al. "Plant-Based Diets Are Associated With a Lower Risk of Incident Cardiovascular Disease, Cardiovascular Disease Mortality, and All-Cause Mortality in a General Population of Middle-Aged Adults." Journal of the American Heart Association 9, no. 22 (2019): e012865. https://doi.org/10.1161/JAHA.119.012865.

16. Todd, Benjamin, and the 80,000 Hours Team. "What Are the Most Pressing World Problems?" 80, 000 Hours, updated June 2025, accessed 18 November 2025, https://80000hours.org/problem-profiles/.

17. Probably Good. "Build a career that's good—for you and for the world." Probably Good, accessed 18 November 2025, https://probablygood.org/.

18. Against Malaria Foundation. Against Malaria Foundation (charity website), accessed 18 November 2025. https://www.againstmalaria.com/.

19. Malaria Consortium. "Who we are." Malaria Consortium US, accessed 18 November 2025, https://www.malariaconsortium.org/mc-us/who-we-are.

20. Helen Keller Intl. "Continuing Her Work." Helen Keller Intl, accessed 18 November 2025. https://helenkellerintl.org/.

21. New Incentives. "Cash transfers that save lives." New Incentives, accessed 18 November 2025, https://www.newincentives.org/.

22. GiveWell. "Our Top Charities." GiveWell, last updated September 2025, accessed 18 November 2025, https://www.givewell.org/charities/top-charities.

23. GiveDirectly. "Send money directly to people who need it most." GiveDirectly, accessed 18 November 2025, https://www.givedirectly.org/.

24. Roser, Max. "How many animals are factory-farmed?" Our World in Data, 2019, accessed 18 November 2025, https://ourworldindata.org/how-many-animals-are-factory-farmed.

25. Animal Charity Evaluators. "Animal Charity Evaluators: Helping People Help Animals." Animal Charity Evaluators, accessed 18 November 2025, https://animalcharityevaluators.org/.

26. The Humane League. "The Humane League." The Humane League, accessed 18 November 2025. https://thehumaneleague.org/.

27. The Good Food Institute. "About." The Good Food Institute, accessed 18 November 2025. https://gfi.org/about/.

28. Material Innovation Initiative. "Advancing the next-gen materials revolution." Material Innovation Initiative, accessed 18 November 2025. https://materialinnovation.org/.

29. Animal Equality. "Animal Equality is an international organization working to end

cruelty to farmed animals." Animal Equality, accessed 18 November 2025, https://animalequality.org/.

30. Anima International. "We help animals effectively using evidence." Anima International, accessed 18 November 2025. https://animainternational.org/.

31. StrongMinds. "StrongMinds democratizes access to mental health care." StrongMinds, accessed 18 November 2025, https://strongminds.org/.

32. Action for Happiness. "Let's take action to be happier and kinder, together." Action for Happiness, accessed 18 November 2025. https://actionforhappiness.org/.

33. Vida Plena. "Building strong mental health in Latin America." Vida Plena, accessed 18 November 2025. https://vidaplena.global/.

34. Bloom Wellbeing Fund. "We think wellbeing is at the heart of what matters." Bloom Wellbeing Fund, accessed 18 November 2025. https://bloomwellbeing.fund/.

35. Mental Health Funders. MentalHealthFunders.com, accessed 18 November 2025. https://www.mentalhealthfunders.com/.

36. Blueprint Biosecurity. "Blueprint Biosecurity is a nonprofit dedicated to achieving breakthroughs in humanity's ability to prevent pandemics." Blueprint Biosecurity, accessed 18 November 2025. https://blueprintbiosecurity.org/.

37. Horizon Institute. "Augmenting global intelligence." Horizon Institute, accessed 18 November 2025. https://www.horizoninstitute.org/.

38. International Biosecurity & Biosafety Initiative for Science (IBBIS). "Safeguarding modern bioscience and biotechnology so it can advance and flourish safely and responsibly." IBBIS, accessed 18 November 2025. https://ibbis.bio/.

39. Nuclear Threat Initiative (NTI). "Biological threats—natural, intentional, or accidental—could kill millions and cost trillions." NTI Biological Threats Program, accessed 18 November 2025. https://www.nti.org/area/biological/.

40. Founders Pledge. "Empowering entrepreneurs to do immense good." Founders Pledge, accessed 18 November 2025. https://www.founderspledge.com/.

41. Center for a New American Security (CNAS). "Artificial Intelligence Safety and Stability." CNAS, accessed 18 November 2025. https://www.cnas.org/artificial-intelligence.

42. Americans for Responsible Innovation. "AI policy advocacy in the public interest." Americans for Responsible Innovation, accessed 18 November 2025. https://www.centerforresponsibleinnovation.org/.

43. Horizon Institute for Public Service. See note 37.

44. Institute for Law & AI. "The Institute for Law and AI is an independent think tank that researches and advises on the legal challenges posed by artificial intelligence." Institute for Law & AI, accessed 18 November 2025. https://law-ai.org/.

45. Effective Institutions Project. "The Effective Institutions Project is a philanthropic advisory and research organization dedicated to strengthening society's ability to tackle major global challenges." Effective Institutions Project, accessed 18 November 2025. https://effectiveinstitutionsproject.org/.

46. FAR.AI. "Ensuring advanced AI is safe and beneficial for everyone." FAR.AI, accessed 18 November 2025. https://far.ai/.
47. Centre for Long-Term Resilience. "Striving for a safe and flourishing world." Long-Term Resilience, accessed 18 November 2025. https://www.longtermresilience.org/.
48. Institute for Development Innovation. "We help leaders design smarter welfare programs that truly deliver for the poorest 300 million Indians." Institute for Development Innovation, accessed 18 November 2025. https://www.idiinstitute.org/.
49. High Impact Professionals. "Free resources." High Impact Professionals, accessed 18 November 2025. https://www.highimpactprofessionals.org/free-resources.
50. Clear, James. "Core Values List: Over 200 Personal Values to Live by." JamesClear.com, accessed 18 November 2025. https://jamesclear.com/core-values.
51. Indeed Editorial Team. "How to Write a Personal Mission Statement (Step-by-Step Guide with Examples)." Indeed Career Guide, updated March 2024, accessed 18 November 2025. https://www.indeed.com/career-advice/career-development/personal-mission-statement-examples.
52. Charity Entrepreneurship Team. "Using a Spreadsheet to Make Good Decisions: Five Examples." Charity Entrepreneurship (blog), 25 November 2016, accessed 18 November 2025. https://www.charityentrepreneurship.com/post/using-a-spreadsheet-to-make-good-decisions-five-examples.
53. Charity Entrepreneurship. Charity Entrepreneurship (website), accessed 18 November 2025. https://www.charityentrepreneurship.com/.
54. Todd, Benjamin. "How to Make Your Career Plan." 80,000 Hours Career Guide (Part 10), May 2023, accessed 18 November 2025. https://80000hours.org/career-guide/career-planning/.
55. High Impact Professionals. See note 49.
56. GiveWell. "How Much Does It Cost to Save a Life?". See note 1.
57. Giving What We Can. "How Rich Am I?" Giving What We Can, accessed 18 November 2025. https://www.givingwhatwecan.org/how-rich-am-i.
58. Killingsworth, Matthew A., Daniel Kahneman, and Barbara Mellers. "Income and Emotional Well-Being: A Conflict Resolved." Proceedings of the National Academy of Sciences 120, no. 10 (2023): e2208661120. https://doi.org/10.1073/pnas.2208661120.
59. Dunn, Elizabeth W., Lara B. Aknin, and Michael I. Norton. "Spending Money on Others Promotes Happiness." Science 319, no. 5870 (2008): 1687–1688. https://greatergood.berkeley.edu/images/uploads/DunnAkninNorton2008.pdf.
60. Aknin, Lara B., Elizabeth W. Dunn, Jordi Proulx, Isabel Lok, and Michael I. Norton. "Does Spending Money on Others Promote Happiness? A Registered Replication Report." Journal of Personality and Social Psychology 119, no. 2 (2020): e15–e26. https://doi.org/10.1037/pspa0000191.

61. World Bank. Poverty and Inequality Platform (PIP). PIP.WorldBank.org, accessed 18 November 2025. https://pip.worldbank.org/.
62. Giving What We Can. "How to Donate Tax-Effectively by Country." Giving What We Can, accessed 18 November 2025. https://www.givingwhatwecan.org/get-involved/tax-deductibility.
63. Giving What We Can. "Turn your income into outcomes." Giving What We Can, accessed 18 November 2025. https://www.givingwhatwecan.org/.
64. Giving What We Can. "The 10% Pledge." Giving What We Can, accessed 18 November 2025. https://www.givingwhatwecan.org/pledge/hip.
65. Founders Pledge. See note 40.
66. Effective Altruism Funds. "Global Health and Development Fund." Effective Altruism Funds, accessed 18 November 2025. https://funds.effectivealtruism.org/funds/global-development.
67. GiveWell. "Top Charities Fund." GiveWell, accessed 18 November 2025. https://www.givewell.org/top-charities-fund.
68. GiveWell. "All Grants Fund." GiveWell, accessed 18 November 2025. https://www.givewell.org/all-grants-fund.
69. Global Health Funders. GlobalHealthFunders.com, accessed 18 November 2025. https://www.globalhealthfunders.com/.
70. Founders Pledge. "Global Health and Development Fund." Founders Pledge, accessed 18 November 2025. https://www.founderspledge.com/funds/global-health-and-development-fund.
71. Effective Altruism Funds. "Animal Welfare Fund." Effective Altruism Funds, accessed 18 November 2025. https://funds.effectivealtruism.org/funds/animal-welfare.
72. Animal Charity Evaluators. "Donate." Animal Charity Evaluators, accessed 18 November 2025. https://animalcharityevaluators.org/donate/.
73. Animal Funding Circle. AnimalFundingCircle.com, accessed 18 November 2025. https://www.animalfundingcircle.com/.
74. Mental Health Funders. See note 35.
75. Bloom Wellbeing Fund. See note 34.
76. Founders Pledge. "Climate Change Fund." Founders Pledge, accessed 18 November 2025. https://www.founderspledge.com/programs/climate-fund/about.
77. Giving Green. "Simplifying Climate Giving." Giving Green, accessed 18 November 2025. https://www.givinggreen.earth/.
78. Effective Altruism Funds. "Long-Term Future Fund." Effective Altruism Funds, accessed 18 November 2025. https://funds.effectivealtruism.org/funds/far-future.
79. Longview Philanthropy. "Emerging Challenges Fund." Longview Philanthropy, accessed 18 November 2025. https://www.longview.org/fund/emerging-challenges-fund/.

80. Effective Altruism Funds. "Effective Altruism Infrastructure Fund." Effective Altruism Funds, accessed 18 November 2025. https://funds.effectivealtruism.org/funds/ea-community.
81. Meta Charity Funders. MetaCharityFunders.com, accessed 18 November 2025. https://www.metacharityfunders.com/.
82. Seed Network Funders. SeedNetworkFunders.com, accessed 18 November 2025. https://www.seednetworkfunders.com/.
83. Charity Entrepreneurship. See note 53.
84. Giving What We Can. "Donor Lottery." Giving What We Can, accessed 18 November 2025. https://www.givingwhatwecan.org/donor-lottery.
85. Giving What We Can. "Leave a Legacy: Bequests." Giving What We Can, accessed 18 November 2025. https://www.givingwhatwecan.org/get-involved/bequests.
86. Founders Pledge. "Patient Philanthropy Fund." Founders Pledge, accessed 18 November 2025. https://www.founderspledge.com/funds/patient-philanthropy-fund.
87. Giving What We Can. See note 57.
88. EA Good Governance Project. EAGoodGovernance.com, accessed 18 November 2025. https://www.eagoodgovernance.com/.
89. Giving What We Can. "Fundraisers." Giving What We Can, accessed 18 November 2025. https://www.givingwhatwecan.org/fundraisers.
90. High Impact Professionals. "Impact Accelerator Program." High Impact Professionals, accessed 18 November 2025. https://www.highimpactprofessionals.org/impact-accelerator-program.
91. Boss as a Service. BossAsAService.com, accessed 18 November 2025. https://bossasaservice.com/.
92. I mean it, here: hipbook@highimpactprofessionals.org.
93. High Impact Professionals. See note 90.
94. Probably Good Jobs Board. jobs.probablygood.org, accessed 18 November 2025. https://jobs.probablygood.org/.
95. 80,000 Hours Job Board. jobs.80000hours.org, accessed 18 November 2025. https://jobs.80000hours.org/.
96. High Impact Professionals. "Find a Job." High Impact Professionals, accessed 18 November 2025. https://www.highimpactprofessionals.org/find-a-job.